# The Power of Enlightenment
*Chinese Zen Poems*

# The Power of Enlightenment
## *Chinese Zen Poems*

WU YANSHENG

TRANSLATED by TONY BLISHEN

Better Link Press

# Contents

## Song Dynasty (960–1279) 131

## Modern and Contemporary (1840–present) 175

## Translator's Postscript 184

# Introduction

In opening this book you will visit the depths of the realms of Zen and of poetry, of the awakened life and of oriental wisdom.

You will transcend time and space and enter the spiritual world of the enlightened. With eyes opened to wisdom you will share with the masters the tranquility, purity, grace and ease of life.

Anxiety will be dispelled, your spirit will aspire to the sublime and your soul will be purified, allowing you to live in this world as would a poet.

### What is Zen?

"Zen" (Chinese *chan*) is a Japanese transliteration of the Sanskrit word "Dhyana" which has the meaning of "calm consideration", "cultivation of thinking" and "assimilation of concepts". In other words, meditation in the sense of the concentration of one's thought on a single point through the practice of seated Zen, thereby precipitating the mind's sediment and clarifying thought so that it is as translucent as water.

Zen is a state that transcends the dualism of opposites to achieve spiritual harmony.

Zen is a method that throws off the fetters of distinctions to achieve freedom of mind.

Zen is a home that brings an end to wandering to achieve

peace of mind.

The Zen Master Laiguo said: "The wisdom of the Buddhas of all places is born from Zen and from calm" (*Sayings of Zen Master Laiguo*). There is a very close connection between Zen and calm. Huineng, the Sixth Patriarch said: "Outwardly to be apart from the appearance of things is Zen, inwardly to be free of confusion is a settled calm (*ding*)" (*Platform Sutra*). Being unmoved by the brilliance of the external world and to transcend form, that is Zen; once having transcended external form and the spirit having preserved its freedom, that is settled calm. Through Zen and settled calm one's concept of life itself may undergo a major change.

## What is Zen Poetry?

Zen is Buddhism and verse is literature. As the name implies, Zen verse is a combination of religion and poetry. A Zen poem bears both the inner meaning of Zen and the characteristics of poetry.

Zen poetry is verse through which practitioners of Zen express the knowledge and experience they have gained of the comprehension, practice, and perception of Zen so as to promote Zen philosophy or to express the spirit of Zen. It has a mystical attraction that contains a deep feeling for mankind, society, nature and the universe. In the broadest sense Zen poetry is the verse of Buddhism. In the narrow sense it is Buddhist verse imbued with the spirit of Zen produced after the introduction of Buddhism to China. The Zen poetry in this book is the poetry of the broad definition. The poems are widely known, long-lived and much loved.

The authors of Zen poetry fall into two categories: Buddhist and Zen monks and those who are neither but who come, in the main, from the ranks of the *literati*, ranging from the emperor and his ministers to the poverty-stricken and beggars.

In terms of numbers, Zen poetry of the broad definition arises from the opportunity presented by the transmission of Buddhism to China during the Han and Jin dynasties. Incomplete statistics suggest a figure of over 30,000 poems, a unique form in the garden of Chinese classical verse.

In content, Zen poetry numbers six kinds: poems of comprehension, of metaphor, of context, of allegory, of practice and of enlightenment.

Since Zen verse is "poetry" it has the characteristics of classical Chinese verse particularly in terms of style, rhythm, and mood. In reality, it does not always completely accord with the stylistic conventions of classical verse but is an improvisation on the basis of Buddhist *gatha* chant or hymns. Because of this custom, *gatha* has also become part of Zen verse. Following the prose narration (long form) of the Buddhist sutras they were summarized again in verse (*gatha*) to reinforce the impression upon the reader. Since *gatha* was much the same in form as verse it was called *gatha* verse or verse-*gatha*. Since it was not strictly limited to verse form it was also known as *gatha* language, *gatha*-writing and *gatha*-speech. Following the spread of Buddhism within China, Buddhist monks and the *literati* liked to use *gatha* to expound the principles of Buddhism and they became simple, lively but deeply moral poems in a much loved form that alternates verse with common speech.

On the basis of the writer's research and experience and seen from the point of view of enlightenment, Zen verse may be divided into six categories: poems of comprehension, of metaphor, of context, of allegory, of practice and of enlightenment. These categories are described below on the basis of the poems selected for inclusion.

## 1. Poems of comprehension

These are poems and *gatha* that explain philosophical methods or express Zen philosophy. They concentrate on the explanation of philosophy. The Zen that is expressed through these poems is the crystallization of the poet's particular points of view on society, life, nature, experience of the universe, of Buddhist contemplation and illumination, and of self-examination. They cover the following:

i) Abandonment of desire. With desire life degenerates into the cycle of re-birth. The practice of Zen first requires the emptying of the mind (*xin kong*) for success. Example: "This is the place of Buddha choice, / Where only minds empty of dust succeed."

ii) Transcending the trammels of a predilection for the world of dust. One lives in the world and although it is difficult to avoid being caught up in the red dust of the mundane, it is the return to one's original nature that is precious. If this is not understood, one becomes enslaved by the outward or external world and enlightenment becomes difficult to attain. Example: "Though I pursued the mundane dust, / I came awake at last. / Those who do not know this truth, / Must labor in lifelong toil."

iii) Understanding one's spiritual home. The basis of the practice of asceticism is discipline of the mind. Whilst cultivation of the physical body is obviously important it is not more important than spiritual cultivation. Example: "Better to nurse the mind / Than the body. / The body is content / With a nourished mind."

iv) Realizing Zen in life. Buddha's law is of this world and enlightenment must be achieved in this world. It cannot be realized by seeking it beyond the world. Example: "Buddha's law is of this world / And not beyond. / To search beyond / Seeks horns upon a rabbit."

v) Acquiring experience of the philosophy of cause. Everything in the world is the result of a combination of causes, in the same way that the beautiful sound of the plucked *qin* arises from the combination of the *qin* string with the fingers. Example: "If the sound of the *qin* / Lies in its strings, / Why is it not heard / Inside the box? / If you say it's in the fingers, / Why don't I hear it from yours?"

vi) Purifying utilitarianism. It is difficult to achieve results by praying with a utilitarian attitude of mind. Success can only come through praying with a pure mind. Example: "Buddhas are few but many chant the prayers. / Through long years of chanting, / They fall to the demon fire."

2. Poems of metaphor

The use of metaphor and analogy to create poems and *gatha* that express the ideals of Zen. The poems emphasize the construction of Zen metaphors including:

i) Metaphors of the impermanence of life. Life ends with the grave and none can escape. The humped graves outside the city wall resemble buns made of earth and their filling the living beings from within the city. Example: "Without the city wall, the graves of earth / Lie humped like steamed buns, / Their filling the stuff of those yet within."

ii) Metaphors of the evanescence of glory. Like a peony in blossom, it is void in the instant, there is no need to wait for it to wither and fall. Example: "Why wait for the fallen blossom / To begin to know the void?" One wakens from dreams and sounds are extinguished, one can only wake from fantasy by seeing through the illusions of life. Examples: "It's always piles of gold / In our dreams. / A greed for wealth and honor / Difficult to curb." "All creation sounds of itself / But space is still forever."

iii) Metaphors of the destruction wreaked by desire. Greed for money can set one upon the path to destruction, like the pot used by the ancients to store money which was smashed the moment it was full. Example: "Just stuffing your belly with cash, / How can you know its harm?"

iv) Metaphors of the overcoming of desire. Practitioners overcome the desire in their hearts in the same way that the higher monks vanquish the poisonous dragons in the pool. Example: "Dusk falls by the empty pool / And Zen stills the dragons of desire."

v) Metaphors of the independence of life and death. The spirit lives in the fleshly body in the same way that a person lives in a house. The wise realize that in life and death, life resembles the glory of the flowers in summer and death the quiet beauty of the leaves in autumn. Example: "My parents built a hut / Where I've lived these eighty years."

vi) Metaphors of release from bondage. Life can be compared to a fly that attempts to get through a window pane to the light but becomes trapped by the window paper. We have to escape in order to achieve spiritual enlightenment, Examples: "Unwilling to leave through an empty door, / Caught in ignorance against the paper window pane." "Suddenly it finds the way it came / And knows itself deceived by life."

vii) Metaphors of advanced practice. The practitioner who reaches the Bodhi of self enlightenment resembles an acrobat sitting on the top of a 100 foot pole, the achievement is great but they must progress further, come to the aid of all sentient beings and bring enlightenment to others. Example: "At the pole top he must exercise more, / To be one with the myriad worlds."

viii) Metaphors of the Mahayana practice of merciful concern for others. Practitioners of Zen cleanse the minds of all sentient beings of filth in the same way that a warm spring washes away the dust from their bodies. Example: "Once all beings are cleansed of dust, / Then clear and cool again, / I'll mingle with the stream once more." Zen practitioners use vigorous methods for eliminating evil from all sentient beings just as woodpeckers peck out the insects that eat trees. Example: "Fail to wake and you'll hear the monk above, / Tock, tock, tocking." Unless the problems of sentient beings are solved there can be no end to the work of the practitioner of Zen.

3. Poems of context

These poems and *gatha* seek to establish a context for the expression of the grace of Buddhism and Zen. They express the state of Zen through the use of striking imagery. They cover the following:

i) Direct presentation. Everything remains as it is, direct

and immediate without the intervention of the concept of logic. In the eyes of Zen, streams, sound, hill and color are all Buddha and manifestations of the body of the law. Example: "If the sound of water is its fluent tongue, / Then the mountain is its tranquil body."

ii) Intuitive. An intuitive comprehension of that which transcends writing and language. Zen imprints itself on the mind and is experienced intuitively. Examples: "There is a truth in all of this, / A mystery for which I lack the words." "My heart is like the autumn moon, / Pure as a pool of limpid blue / That nothing can compare. / Teach me what words there are / That can express it."

iii) Conflation. Everything in the natural world is a single complete entity that forms a cosmic life filled with vitality. Examples: "From the east the streams run west to mingle / And from southern hills rise northern clouds. / Flowers bloom in front / But at rear are seen. / Bells above are heard below." "From the eastern temple I see the western temple snow, / From the spring above flows the stream below."

iv) The everyday. Eating and sleeping, drawing water and collecting firewood. They appear insignificant but they have mystic powers. Example: "Enlightenment's mystic power / Is drawing water and hewing wood."

v) Seclusion. Scenes of tranquility. Paths that meander through bamboo to secluded spots. Tranquil Zen huts amidst a deep profusion of flowers and trees appear to the person in the chaotic world of red dust like a world in which the mind is transported to an other-worldly fairy tale garden of peach blossom. Examples: "Through the bamboos a secluded path winds / To a Zen court in depths of flowers and trees." "At dusk I took the down-hill path, / And heard the sound of spring water, / Parting with regret."

vi) Transcendentalist. Flowers bloom and wither, the water in the stream flows away, the hills are unhurried and unchanged, disturbed by nothing. Everything is impermanent, one's nature is motionless. Realization of self brings further transcendence. Example: "When all the flowers have fallen, / The hill remains there still, / The streams themselves flow on, / The hill itself at ease."

vii) The here and now. Living in the present with no obstacles to the mind and where it is possible to enjoy the beauty of the world. Example: "Spring flowers and autumn moon, / Summer breeze and winter snow. / An unencumbered mind / Is man's best season."

viii) Unity. You are one with the pine, you are the pine and the pine is you. A gentle breeze moves the pines producing a beautiful sound and you feel that the breeze has brushed every inch of your skin. Example: "A zephyr gently sighs between the pines, / Its sound more closely heard the better."

ix) The flow of cause. Following the flow of cause and enjoying the delights of the process of living. To have not caught any fish but to return with a boat laden with the full moon is also a joy and a delight. Example: "In the chill water at quiet of night, / No fish seize the bait / But the boat rows home / Loaded with the gleaming moon." Walking in the countryside and chatting happily with an old man met by chance so that you forget to go home. Example: "And talk and laugh beyond the hour / With a forest ancient met by chance."

x) Equability. To be surprised neither by favor nor disgrace and to be able to come and go without mishap is life's greatest comfort. It is like a magnolia that grows by a hut near a stream remote from human habitation, calmly blooming and then gently bowing out. Example: "And by the mountain's lonely torrent, / One by one they bloom, / Then fall."

## 4. Poems of allegory

Poems and *gatha* that use pointed phrases that stimulate the senses to express the essence of Zen. The original meaning of "point" (*jifeng*) referred to the catch (*ji*) and arrow tips (*feng*) of a crossbow, used in Zen as a metaphor for quick-witted and perceptive thought or phrases. Poems of allegory contain more implicit significance than the directness of poems of context, and prompt reflection. They include the following:

i) Zen allegories of the eternal nature of the Buddhist law. There is a limit to the profane world, the life of the flesh is impermanent. Only a life of wisdom will enable you to transcend time and space and live in time. Example: "I sighed that spring had left no trace, / Not knowing that it lingered here."

ii) Allegories of changes of state to the mind. If the mind is at peace so is all else, if the mind is pure all else is at rest. As long as the mind is elevated the clatter of horse and cart will be inaudible even in the marketplace. Example: "I've built my hut amidst this world of men, / Yet without the clatter of horse and cart." If the mind is at ease there is no difference between the sounds of the marketplace and those of a mountain stream. Example: "If the mind's at ease so is all, / In market place or mountain stream."

iii) Allegories of common identity (existence and non-existence exist mutually and each appears more brilliant in the other's company). Zen is, at the same time, both the extreme of immobility within the extreme of mobility and vice-versa. It is non-existence within existence and existence within non-existence. At a place where water has been exhausted, appearance is void, but as you sit and look at the clouds the reverse is true. Example: "To water's head and seated watch the furling clouds."

iv) Allegories of the indivisible and all-embracing nature of the Buddha. The true practitioner is not concerned whether the environment in which he practices is a monastery or the common world. As long as his Zen purpose is firm he can just as well achieve enlightenment and become a Buddha in an ordinary household. Example: "Who can say that living thus obstructs the way? / I take the hermit Weimo as my guide."

v) Allegories of contentment in the here and now. The essence of Zen is to have a grasp of the present and to live in the here and now. If it is cloud then adopt the stance of a cloud and float free in the sky; if it is water, then adopt the position of water, free and at ease in a vase. Example: "I ask the master to show the way, / Without a word, he points to the clouds in the sky / And the water in the vase."

vi) Allegorical answers that are not answers. A practitioner of Zen who places worldly things beyond consideration, may, if he hears a worldly topic, start up a fisherman's song and row the boat towards the deep recesses of the riverbank. Example: "If you ask where lies the meaning in this, / I sing a fisherman's song / And row for the shore."

5. Poems of practice

Poems that refer to skill and achievement in the practice of the attainment of Zen such as:

i) The practice of constant and diligent gradual sweeping

clean. The maintenance of spiritual purity calls for the unceasing practice of the triple theory of discipline, order and wisdom, (the triple theory is an ordered gradual progress in which moral character is first perfected, followed by attempts to order and calm the mind and once that is achieved by progression to an increase in knowledge and wisdom) so that life is purified and not subject to the contamination of the world of dust. Example: "The body is a bodhi tree / And the spirit the bright mirror and its stand, / Polished and swept / Clean of the dust of the world." The attainment of Buddha-hood calls for assiduous practice in order to achieve success. Example: "Without the cold that cuts the bone, / No scent from the blossoming plum / Ever greets the nostrils."

ii) Practice in which the way is everywhere made manifest. The changes in nature, and the beginning and extinction of life are both manifestations of functions of the way. Practice is a continuous realization of the way itself. Example: "Master of all things, / Untouched by the changing seasons."

iii) Practice in ridding the mind of distinctions. Life is born painfully of distinctions. Once rid of them one can feel the vastness of the earth, limpid as a blue pool, and life suddenly takes on a different aspect. Examples: "Knock out the bottom of the barrel / To see the world's extent. / Sever the roots of life / And see the clear blue pool." "Do not test me with tales of right and wrong, / I have no truck with the floating life / Of forced fact and this and that." "Zen has no need for cool hills or water, / Quench the fires of notion within, / And you will be cool enough." "Empty-handed I grasp a hoe, / On foot I ride a buffalo. / Crossing the stream, / It's the bridge that flows, / Not the water."

iv) Practice in an attitude of resolute calm towards the world of dust. Practitioners must be able to resist the temptations of the world of dust. They must defeat vexation and ignorance before achieving a state of Zen calm. Example: "Rouse yourself to gain Zen calm / It's as deep as the sleep / Of a silkworm."

v) Practice in dealing with eroticism through Zen. The privacy of feelings between the sexes resembles the way in which the state of Zen enlightenment cannot be described in words. Example: "This romance of youth / Only one beauty knows."

vi) Rooting out love from the field of emotion. The practitioner has to eradicate human affection before being able to resist the attractions of beauty. Examples: "Like a mud laden willow frond, / My Zen mind does not dance / To the spring wind's jaunty tune." "With a heartless tear I replied, / Why did we not meet / Before my monkish head was shaved?"

vii) Practice in seeking the Buddha-nature within. The way is not further than the person and should be sought within. The more it is sought without the more distant it becomes. To search for it en route is an absurdity. Examples: "Exhausted I return, / And smiling caress a flower, / To breathe the plum blossom's scent, / And find spring ten parts full / At the tip of a stem." "Search not elsewhere, / It is too far from self." "Sought in confusion in the past, / Now found like ice within a fire."

viii) Not dwelling upon an aspect of something and forming an attachment to the detriment of enlightenment. On the one hand the practitioner does not form attachments to external objects and on the other avoids a spiritual response to them. Things come so let them come, and things go so let them go. It is merely a matter of feeling. Example: "To have a heart like that tree, / Would not offend the way."

6. Poems of enlightenment

Poems or *gatha* about the realization of enlightenment that express the calm non-conceptual acceptance of enlightenment.

i) Mind-only perception of phenomena. One's nature gives life to all phenomena and vice-versa. All is the self-mind and the self-mind is all. Example: "There's nothing that lies beyond the mind, / Its eyes filled / With the blue of hills."

ii) The perception of empty by nature (that is, emptiness). The Mahayana concept of emptiness is the gate that leads upwards to instant Buddha-hood and enlightenment. Example: "There was no tree to the bodhi, / Nor yet that bright mirror. / The beginning had no substance, / Where then was the dust?"

iii) Evidence of the innate character of the Zen mind. Unlike the ordinary person, the advanced practitioner who achieves a high level of skill does not need to practice deep breathing, reciting the titles of the Buddha or chanting in order to suppress vain hopes. No such hopes exist at all. Example: "Delusions depart un-banished. / And I am free from distraction."

iv) Enlightenment is everywhere. The practitioner may achieve a flash of enlightenment beneath the peach blossom, as a glass hits the ground, or under any circumstances. Examples: "But now I've seen the peach tree bloom, / I do not doubt at all." "The void too shatters / And wanton desires expire."

v) The similarity of life and death. Life and death are

phenomena. In essence there is neither life nor extinction. The practitioner does not fear death and feels rather that it is the return of the wandering child to its home. The flowers blossom with the sense of spring and the moon hangs full in the sky. This place of limitless tranquility, peace and perfection is life's final destination. Example: "Flowering twigs blossom with the sense of spring / And the heavens so clear that the rounded moon grows larger."

vi) Evidence of the three states of Zen. From the first stage of seeing mountains as mountains and water as water, through the stage of seeing mountains as not mountains and water as not water to the third stage of seeing mountains as mountains and water as water when finally, the possession of a pure mind enables the calm enjoyment of the beauty of all in heaven and earth. Example: "The mists on Lushan and the Zhe river tide. / Before I saw them I felt regret. / Now I've seen them my mind's at rest, / The mists on Lushan and the Zhe river tide."

vii) Evidence of the concept of once in a lifetime. Treasure the opportunities of each moment and make every effort because each encounter may be the only one of a lifetime. Example: "In parting at the temple gate, / Each bamboo leaf / Rustled its own cool breeze."

viii) Evidence of the eternal nature of the Buddha-nature. Neither born nor extinct. Like something that has never withered. Example: "Now back in the place where red flowers were, / I see flowers flowering red once more."

*The Beauty of Zen Verse*

Zen verse is an area of practice where the practitioner

displays the allegories of Zen and testifies to the Buddhist way. It opens the eyes to the wisdom of life and it can help us transcend the corruption and clamor of the world of dust, stimulating the positive energy within us and returning us to spiritual calm and happiness. Zen verse with its lasting appeal, its ethereal quality, carries us away and causes us to reflect.

1. The beauty of the spellbinding: striking metaphors and vivid directness of expression

Zen enlightenment is a profound and penetrating experience that is difficult to convey in words. Poetry is the art of emotional imagery. When poetry conveys Zen enlightenment that can only be sensed that is the best combination of both. The majority of Zen poems included in this book are ones of vivid metaphor. The imagery of these metaphors is exceptional, the implications are cautionary and they are finely wrought and artistically inspiring. For example:

Metaphors of the successive stages in the practice of Zen, where the gradual or sudden process of enlightenment is represented, "Polished and swept" (Shenxiu), "The beginning had no substance" (Huineng).

Metaphors of the search for truth. The search for spring as a metaphor for the process of the search for the way. Example: "Treading in straw sandals / Amid the cloud set peaks, / Searching all day for the spring / I could not find."

Metaphors of the impermanence of things. Using the rise and fall of sound in the air as a metaphor for the change from the flourishing to decline. Example: "All creation sounds of itself / But space is still forever." Using awakening from a dream of riches to poverty as a metaphor for the inevitable void that awaits life's dreams. Example: "It's always piles of gold / In our dreams. / A greed for wealth and honor / Difficult to curb." Using the emptiness of admiring a peony in bloom as a metaphor for the emptiness of the luxuriance that resembles sand. Example: "Why wait for the fallen blossom / To begin to know the void?" Using a goose's footprint in the snow as a metaphor for the transience of human life. Example: "In all, what does life resemble? / It seems a goose print in the slush of snow." Using buns of earth as a metaphor for life's final destination. Example: "Without the city wall, the graves of earth / Lie humped like steamed buns, / Their filling the stuff of those yet within."

Metaphors of the eternal nature of Buddhism. Using "The peach blossom opens in the temple in the hills" as a metaphor for the evergreen nature of Buddhist teaching. Example: "I sighed that spring had left no trace, / Not knowing that it lingered here." Using red flowers as a metaphor for the perpetuity of Buddhism. Examples: "Where flowers flower red, year on year." "I see flowers flowering red once more."

Metaphors of the spirit of the Mahayana (Great Vehicle). Using the hot spring washing away dirt as a metaphor for the purification of the people of the world by the practitioners of Zen. Example: "Once all beings are cleansed of dust, / Then clear and cool again, / I'll mingle with the stream once more." Using the woodpecker's eating of insects as a metaphor for the way in which Zen Masters rid all sentient beings of evil. Example: "Tock, tock, tock. / An insect's inside, / And there's pecking outside."

Metaphors of the strength of settled calm. The use of the metaphor of the hibernating silkworm to describe the depth of skill in achieving settled calm. Example: "Rouse yourself

to gain Zen calm / It's as deep as the sleep / Of a silkworm."
Using the metaphor of the dampened pussy-willow unable
to float in the air to describe the Zen mind that cannot be
provoked by the desires of the mundane world. Example:
"Like a mud laden willow frond, / My Zen mind does not
dance / To the spring wind's jaunty tune."

## 2. Seclusion and tranquility: the nature of self-cultivation

The majority of the descriptions of the quality of forest
and mountain scenes of seclusion and tranquility in Zen
poetry evoke the Zen qualities of remoteness and depth. They
demonstrate a mindset that is tranquil and not self-seeking.

A twisting path threads its way through bamboos to
a remote and tranquil Zen hut surrounded by a profusion
of flowers and trees. Example: "Through the bamboos a
secluded path winds / To a Zen court in depths of flowers
and trees." A gentle breeze blows amongst the remote pines.
As you approach it you become one with it and you can feel
the wonder of the sound as it increases. Example: "A zephyr
gently sighs between the pines / Its sound more closely heard
the better." As you descend the mountain after having visited
a Zen Master's place of retreat, your mind feels like water
from a spring that regrets its parting from the blue of the
mountains. Example: "At dusk I took the down-hill path, /
And heard the sound of spring water, / Parting with regret."
The mountain flowers wither and the mountain streams flow
away but the mountains themselves remain uninfluenced and
retain an air of deep-seated and leisurely calm. Example:
"When all the flowers have fallen, / The hill remains there
still, / The streams themselves flow on, / The hill itself at
ease." Scenic spots of this sort are the best of all places for

nurturing the Zen mind.

3. The beauty of conflation: melding in harmony, harmony above all

The suffering of mankind arises from distinction, delusion and attachment. Consequently, in order to achieve mental tranquility and happiness, the concept of distinction has to be eradicated through the practice of Zen and the use of "The ultimate gateway that transcends all". The beauty of conflation lies in the eradication of the mental attitude that harbors the concept of distinction.

The conflation of the mundane world of red dust with the realm of Zen. Secluded surroundings are extremely important to the practitioner of Zen. Not every practitioner of Zen, however, lives in such surroundings. Hence, the key is to eradicate the mental distinctions between seclusion and clamor and then to conflate the two. Once the mind is at ease it can accept the sense of Zen in its unhurried tranquility whether amidst the clamor of the markets of dust or in the seclusion of the mountain stream. Example: "If the mind's at ease so is all, / In market place or mountain stream."

The conflation of leaving home to seek enlightenment with remaining at home. From the point of view of the capacity for the practice of Zen, there is less disturbance and the conditions are better in leaving home. But if the mind aspires to the diligent practice of Zen, even if one remains at home or is forced to return to the mundane world, it need not influence progress in self-cultivation. Example: "Who can say that living thus obstructs the way? / I take the hermit Weimo as my guide."

The conflation of vexation with bodhi. The possession of

27

a sense of distinction is a vexation and anxiety, and ridding oneself of it is bodhi, enlightenment. The practice of Zen is the elimination of all opposites so that even amongst vexation and anxiety one may have the ease of bodhi. Example: "Zen has no need for cool hills or water, / Quench the fires of notion within, / And you will be cool enough."

The conflation of life with death. The common feeling of the mundane world is of an attachment to the corporeal life. It is greedy for life and fears death. From the Buddhist point of view, the body is merely accommodation provided for us by our mother and father (example: My parents built a hut / Where I've lived these eighty years.) which inevitably becomes damaged after being lived in for so long. The conclusion of physical life in this world is, in fact, a return to one's original nature. The flower twigs blossom and are filled with the sense of spring, the heavens are bright with the fullness of the moon, it is the homecoming of the physical body. Example: "Flowering twigs blossom with the sense of spring / And the heavens so clear that the rounded moon grows larger."

The conflation of the four seasons. Each time and season has its own unique qualities to be seized and enjoyed. The spring flowers and the autumn moon are obviously beautiful but the cool breeze in summer and the snowscapes of winter are also beautiful beyond imagination. The key is that one's mind should have a conflated sense of the goodness in each day. Example: "Spring flowers and autumn moon, / Summer breeze and winter snow."

Conflation of the four points of the compass. Each place and point of the compass also has its own unique quality. The universe as a whole is a single vibrant meld of life. The practitioner of Zen can experience the beauty of life in the flow of water, the blending of the clouds, the contrasts of the flowers and the mutual audibility of the sound of bells. Example: "From the east the streams run west to mingle / And from southern hills rise northern clouds. / Flowers bloom in front / But at rear are seen. / Bells above are heard below."

4. The quality of being at ease: following the course of affinity and fate, living in the present

Following the flow of predestined affinity, calmly facing fate and living contentedly in the present. When spirits are high, moving forward alone. Enjoying to the utmost things that are of especial beauty. Example: "When fancy strikes, I stroll alone, / Drunk with joy of sight and sound." Meeting by chance somebody with whom there is an affinity and laughing and talking and forgetting the time to return. Example: "And talk and laugh beyond the hour / With a forest ancient met by chance." Failing to catch fish but returning home with a boat loaded with the bright moon can also cause joy. Example: "In the chill water at quiet of night, / No fish seize the bait / But the boat rows home / Loaded with the gleaming moon." At the end of a tea party, the reluctant farewell wave of the bamboo fronds dancing in the breeze by the entrance as the host says goodbye to his guests at the door. Example: "In parting at the temple gate, / Each bamboo leaf / Rustled its own cool breeze." The life of a practitioner is like a magnolia that grows by a hut near a stream remote from human habitation, it blooms when it blooms and withers when it withers, neither happy nor sad, calmly accepting all the circumstances of life. Example: "And by the mountain's lonely torrent, / One by one they bloom, / Then fall."

5. The beauty of penetrating clarity: freedom from desire, utterly at ease

The pure spirit is not infected by any vexation and remains utterly unaffected.

Everything is of the self-mind and the self-mind is everything. Example: "There's nothing that lies beyond the mind, / Its eyes filled / With the blue of hills." When the consciousness becomes infected by the concept of opposites it is impossible to see one's original appearance. At the moment of enlightenment the dust of the concept of names and appearances, of the visible, is swept away and there is a return instead to the state of the absolute before the intervention of consciousness and a return to the immutable dust of the blue mountains unpolluted by the mundane world. Example: "Scarlet and purple differ but in name, / No dust stains the hills." Zen practitioners long immersed in the way to enlightenment, single-minded and devoted, will, when the time of cause and affinity is ripe, have their ignorance shattered and be able to achieve instant enlightenment through the sound of a handful of gravel striking bamboo or the sound of a glass smashing on the ground. Example: "A tea bowl falls and smashes / Like a thunderclap. / The void too shatters / And wanton desires expire." In the instant of enlightenment all delusions vanish without trace as if of their own accord, without the need for a laborious fundamental rooting out. Example: "Delusions depart un-banished. / And I am free from distraction." Moreover, after enlightenment has been achieved the practitioner will have unlimited confidence in this experience. Example: "But now I've seen the peach tree bloom, / I do not doubt at all."

6. The beauty of the absence of words

Zen enlightenment is an internal experience, a beauty not easy to express and that cannot be represented in words, "There is a truth in all of this, / A mystery for which I lack the words." In much the same way that at the Meeting at Mount Lingshan, Sakyamuni Buddha took the flower and Mahakasyapa, his heart filled with enlightenment, broke into a smile, enlightened in mind and spirit, mind and consciousness at one without the need for words.

In describing the moment of enlightenment phrases such as "heart like the autumn moon" or "like the limpid blue pool" are clever and convenient similes. In fact there is fundamentally no external object that may be used as a simile for enlightenment. A simile is merely to show the finger that points at the moon. Example: "That nothing can compare. / Teach me what words there are / That can express it." When the poet faces the southern hills holding a cup of wine, all words become superfluous. Example: "Without a companion I come / And toast the southern hills alone." The way is the clouds in the sky as they change shape in the wind, the water calmly at ease in a vase. The use of words can only damage them. Example: "I ask the master to show the way, / Without a word, he points to the clouds in the sky / And the water in the vase." The practitioner is unconcerned with the world of dust and takes no heed of its rights and wrongs. Example: "Do not test me with tales of right and wrong, / I have no truck with the floating life / Of forced fact and this and that." If he meets someone who asks him these kinds of question he simply disposes of it by using the answer that does not answer. Example: "If you ask where lies the meaning in this, / I sing a fisherman's song / And row for the shore."

## Criteria for Inclusion

This book contains 66 classic Chinese Zen poems. The sole qualification for inclusion has been depth of feeling and understanding. Each poem indicates a state that transcends the dualism of opposites to achieve spiritual harmony, a method that throws off the fetters of distinctions to achieve freedom of mind and a home that brings an end to wandering to achieve peace of mind.

The book also introduces and provides insights into the Zen spirit of each poem and of its author in the hope that it will assist the reader towards the realms of Zen and of poetry. These poems are a gathering together of the essence of classical Zen poetry and represent its highest achievement. Their language is vivid, their similes surprisingly original and their mood ethereal. The poetry of Zen is intellectually stimulating and agile. It leads people onwards and upwards and gives cause for thought. It does not suffer from being read over and over again. Consequently, Zen poems remain well loved and enduring.

Wang Guowei in his *Sayings of This World* wrote: "Time and again you may seek that other one amongst the multitudes and suddenly look back and see that he stands in the fading light of the lamp." That other, for whom there has been a difficult and arduous search, is one's original nature, the way, the Buddha-nature. In reading this book you may discover to your delight that after an arduous search you will finally find the ultimate hopes that lie in the depths of your spirit.

Please now enter this book with a calm mind and walk, arm in arm with the Masters, in the world of enlightenment.

# Wei, Jin and Northern and Southern Dynasties

## (220–581)

# 1

## Drinking Wine
### *Tao Yuanming*

*I've built my hut amidst this world of men,*
*Yet without the clatter of horse and cart.*
*If you asked how could that be?*
*I'd say I float distant from this dusty world,*
*I pluck the chrysanthemum bloom beneath*
  *the eastern fence,*
*And see serene the southern hills.*
*The hills glow at day's end light,*
*And chattering birds seek their nest.*
*There is a truth in all of this,*
*A mystery for which I lack the words.*

In the midst of the vulgar world the practitioner of Zen remains carefree and untouched by the dust of the mundane. Amongst all its bustle and clamor he uses his mind to transport himself to another realm where he can concentrate on the profound. He is at ease and at one with nature; in achievement he returns to his original nature and transcends the every-day and ordinary; in practice and experience he is instinctively aware of the fundamentals of life.

A sense of Zen Buddhism already existed in China before the arrival of the Buddhist law (Dharma). This poem expresses the author's aspirations for a state of detachment, his intimate love for nature and his style of unhurried contentment and broad spiritual understanding. The poem can be taken as representative of Zen verse of the early period, a fine example that truly embodies the spirit of Zen. The poem does not mention the word Zen but it is suffused with Zen and compared with the majority of Zen verse is more poetic and conveys a greater sense of Zen.

**Tao Yuanming**, c.365 or 372–427, style name Yuanliang. His father died early and as he was from a poor family he pursued a career as an official. Because of his upright character he was unwilling to curry favor with those in power and resigned to follow instead a life of self-sufficient rural simplicity. Nevertheless, he was content in poverty and happy in pursuit of the way (*dao*). He was much esteemed by later generations and was known as the ancestor of hermetic poetry.

# 2
## Before Heaven and Earth
### *Fu Xi*

*Before Heaven and Earth,*
                   *——Matter.*
*Formless and solitary,*
*Master of all things,*
*Untouched by the changing seasons.*

Fu Xi's life was one of colorful legend. On one occasion at court, he was wearing a Daoist cap, a Buddhist *kasaya* and a pair of Confucian shoes. The emperor asked: "Are you a Buddhist monk?" Fu Xi pointed at his cap. "Are you a Daoist then?" Fu Xi pointed at his Confucian shoes. "Are you a commoner?" Fu Xi indicated the *kasaya* draped over his shoulder and left. To this day, statues of Fu Xi portray him wearing all three of these items. In fact, Fu Xi's actions expressed, in physical form, the spirit of Chinese Zen: at bottom Confucian, at top Daoist and Buddhist at heart, embodying a meld of Confucianism, Daoism and Buddhism.

Borrowing the meaning of a phrase from Laozi's *Daodejing* "There was inchoate matter, created before heaven and earth. It was formless and of itself, alone and unchanging", this poem describes the inherent, invisible character of the way. All changes in creation, birth and extinction are connected inextricably to this "way" and are manifestations of its function but can have no influence upon its fundamental nature. As long as we do not form attachments to the outward, external aspect of things, we can return to our original source and see our Buddha-nature. We become masters of our own lives, living full independent lives of purity, stability, fortune, joy and health…to comprehend this is to enter the gates of Zen.

**Fu Xi**, 497–569, also known as Master Shanhui, well-known Zen master of the Kingdom of Liang of the Northern and Southern Dynasties.

# 3

## Grasping a Hoe Empty-Handed
### *Fu Xi*

*Empty-handed I grasp a hoe,*
*On foot I ride a buffalo.*
*Crossing the stream,*
*It's the bridge that flows,*
*Not the water.*

It is said that the outstanding brilliance of Chinese Zen is
to be found in the way in which it transcends logic and
smashes through the inertia of our thinking. This poem is a
fine example.

This *gatha* appears extraordinarily abstruse, and at first
makes us feel as if we are standing on our head, ridiculous
and illogical. How can an "empty hand" "grasp a hoe"? How
can "on foot" be "riding a buffalo"? How can it be that "It's
the bridge that flows, not the water"?

In this *gatha* the poet deliberately juxtaposes the
contradictory images of the empty hand with the hand
that grasps the hoe, the person on foot with the buffalo
rider and the flowing bridge with the still water and forces
our thinking towards an untenable position where it is
impossible to hold on to the concept of distinctions. It
is only when you reach such a position that it is possible

to shatter all the concepts and ideas of distinction that occupy the mind. It is the possession of the idea of such opposites as suffering and joy, sorrow and happiness that has produced ignorance, delusion and vexation, so that fundamentally ridding our consciousness of its deep-rooted concepts of distinction can bring us to a wise and fulfilled comprehension of the problems of self and other, praise and vilification, adverse and favorable circumstances and life and death.

If you stop your habitual thinking in its tracks, turn aside from logic and look back, you will see Zen and enlightenment waiting for you.

# Tang Dynasty
## (618–907)

# 4

## Steamed Buns of Earth Beyond the City Wall
### *Wang Fanzhi*

*Without the city wall, the graves of earth*
*Lie humped like steamed buns,*
*Their filling the stuff of those yet within.*
*One each—its taste inevitable.*

No matter how rich, distinguished or glorious you may
have been in life, like an "earthen steamed bun" you will
be abandoned outside the city walls after death. Moreover,
whether or not you like eating these buns, you will have to
eat one in the end, and you yourself are the filling! Even
if life within the steamed bun lacks flavor, you are obliged
to obediently choose it without complaining that it lacks
taste!

The moral of this poem is an ear-splitting admonition.
Since the graves are earthen buns those in the graves
must be the meat filling for the buns. Obviously it is the
dead who will become meat filling in the future, and the
dead are clearly pursuing success "within" (the city wall)!
Reading this may strike a chill in the hearts of a generation
that pursues success.

**Wang Fanzhi**, early Tang monk who wrote poetry in

the vernacular language. Based on Buddhist doctrine, his poetry generally exhorted people to righteous behavior and the avoidance of evil. He was scathing about the state of the world and his language was plain but humorous. There was always a philosophical element to his ridicule.

# 5

## Living in Peace

*Han Shan*

*If you seek to dwell in peace,*
*Cold Mountain is the place.*
*A zephyr gently sighs between the pines,*
*Its sound more closely heard the better.*
*Beneath the pines an old white-beard*
*Mumbles the words of Huang and Lao,*
*Alone a decade here without return.*
*Forgotten now,*
*The path by which he came.*

Whether it be Confucian self-cultivation, the Way of the Daoists or the Zen practices of Buddhism, there are two routes, one through the inner mind and the other by way of the external environment. "Dwell in peace" suggests the external environment.

The gentle breeze moves the tranquil pines with a mysterious sound, and the closer you are the more joyfully it falls upon the ears. How can this sound be "more closely heard"? Mere physical proximity is insufficient, you must approach it spiritually, enter it and become one with it. You are the pine and the pine is you. At this point you may feel that a kind breeze has brushed over each pine twig of your skin so that your heart is filled with joy and you exclaim: "Oh, this is the life of tranquility, of joy, and of mystery!"

When you are distant from the red dust of the mundane world then you can be close to nature and become the pine, the breeze, a flower, a leaf or a dewdrop.

Those who cultivate themselves in surroundings of such beauty are fortunate indeed. See, beneath the pines, the old white-beard reciting to himself the self-improving texts of Laozi and the Yellow Emperor. What a wonderful experience!

It is easy to achieve a settled calm (*ding*) when the mind is free of distraction. This ancient practitioner solemnly achieved calm through study. Where did he come from? And what happened in the red dust of the mundane world? He is already immersed in the process of enlightenment and has forgotten the way back to the world of red dust. He has already abandoned that which ought to be abandoned and forgotten that which must be forgotten. Forgetting the past and harboring no delusions about the future is the only way of living happily and realistically in the present.

**Han Shan**, well known Tang dynasty monk-poet. As a child he enjoyed the life of a rich family. As a young man, he took the imperial examinations several times unsuccessfully and returned home in chagrin. During his stay in the capital he had become a bookish drifter. Because of his inability to achieve honor in the ordinary world he wandered the country with bitter memories and finally chose to become a hermit. Historically, even his real name remains unknown and all that is left is the name Han Shan (Cold Mountain) and a collection of poems—*Collected Poems of Han Shan*.

During the May 4th movement of 1919, the Chinese literary world began to vigorously encourage literature in Modern Chinese and Han Shan's style received favorable attention. From the 1950s on, Han Shan's poetry crossed to America where the beat generation made him an idol and he became a patriarch of the hippy movement. His poetry is popular in Europe and America and has been translated into English and French for a mass readership.

His poetry of seclusion and of Zen is the most precious, whilst the Zen beauty embodied in his scenic poetry is difficult to attain. His unique style was imitated by later generations and became the characteristic "Han Shan form".

# 6
## My Heart Is Like the Autumn Moon
*Han Shan*

*My heart is like the autumn moon,*
*Pure as a pool of limpid blue*
*That nothing can compare.*
*Teach me what words there are*
*That can express it.*

Laozi said: "The way (*dao*) that is susceptible to logic is
not eternal. Nor is a name that can be named eternal." The
great way (*da dao*) is capable of expression but not through
normal means. Names may be used to nominate but they
are not the general run of name.

The great masters of Zen frequently use the bright
moon as a metaphor for the enlightened mind or heart.
Thus, the "my heart" of the poem refers to an enlightened
heart, one that resembles the autumn moon, refulgent
and free of distractions. At the moment of enlightenment
the rays of wisdom illuminate the world. This heart
shines on the clear tranquility of the water of the pool so
that moon and water meld into a manifestation of purity.
This is to use the autumn moon to represent one's own
heart and to use the contrast between the limpidity of the
pool and the autumn moon to describe the brightness of

the enlightened heart.

Zen practitioners say: "In the waters of a thousand rivers there is a moon to each." The moon shines upon a thousand rivers and a thousand rivers reflect a single moon. In reality, the moon shines upon more than just the water of the pool, or in the river. It shines, too, upon the ranges of hills, the valleys and upon the earth. Although the shining purity of the moon and the pool are used as a metaphor for the enlightened heart, the metaphor is not totally apt because there really is no language that can match the spirit enlightened by Zen. No matter what simile or comparison is employed it is difficult to express the shining purity of the heart that the author describes! He would like to describe it but there is no way that he can do so in words.

The true Zen experience is like the dumb eating honey. The sweetness within the heart resembles "instinctively distinguishing hot and cold when drinking water". The flavor of the state of enlightenment can only be known through experience.

# 7

# The Body Is a Bodhi Tree
## *Shenxiu*

*The body is a bodhi tree*
*And the spirit the bright mirror and its stand,*
*Polished and swept*
*Clean of the dust of the world.*

The bodhi is an evergreen tree under whose branches
Sakyamuni is reputed to have achieved enlightenment. This
single verse describes how the body is the foundation for
the practice of spiritual cultivation and must therefore be
scrupulously maintained and disciplined. A body mired in
desire will have difficulty in sustaining a pure and tranquil
soul.

A mirror stands upon a cosmetics box and is
consequently called a mirror stand (*ming jing tai*). The
woman devoted to her appearance keeps her mirror stand
carefully arranged and spotlessly clean. The analogy here is
between the need for spotlessness of the mirror stand and
the need to maintain purity of spirit.

How do we purify our body and soul? Our bodies and
souls are defiled by the three poisons of greed, anger, and
delusion. They must be purified by the triple theory of
discipline, order and wisdom. A life swept clean of dust is a

life of purity and enlightenment. The mind and spirit is the key to cultivation, thus, the mirror stand must be dusted often so that when the six roots of sight, hearing, taste, speech, touch and thought come into contact with their six antithetical dusts, they are not defiled.

Through the analogy of form, this *gatha* shows the importance of continuous long-term spiritual cultivation. Hongren, the Fifth Patriarch, when he came to choose a successor, asked his disciples to each compose a *gatha* from which he would choose one. Shenxiu composed this one which became the symbol of the Northern School of Zen. However, when Hongren looked at it, he considered that Shenxiu had only reached the threshold of spiritual cultivation and had not ascended into the hall. Thus, he did not bestow his *kasaya* upon him but upon Huineng, the composer of the following *gatha*.

**Shenxiu**, 606–706, founder of the Northern School of Chinese Zen and known as its Sixth Patriarch. Studied Confucianism when young and was a man of considerable learning. Subsequently became a Buddhist monk under the Fifth Patriarch Master Hongren who regarded him highly. At the age of over 90 received an imperial summons to preach Buddhism in the capital where he was revered by the empress Wu Zetian and the emperors Zhongzong and Ruizong of the Tang dynasty, being known as "Teacher to Three Emperors".

# 8
## There Was No Tree to the Bodhi
### *Huineng*

*There was no tree to the bodhi,*
*Nor yet that bright mirror.*
*The beginning had no substance,*
*Where then was the dust?*

Shenxiu's *gatha* was written on the wall of the south
cloister of his Buddhist monastery. Having heard it being
recited, Huineng considered that Shenxiu's proposition had
not reached the state of Buddha-hood and that he would
have some difficulty in becoming a Buddha. He then asked
somebody to write his own *gatha* on the wall. This was the
direct opposite of Shenxiu's proposition and embodied
Huineng's concept of enlightenment in the instant and
"the emptiness of the teaching of the law" and became
the theoretical basis upon which the aims of the Southern
Zen School were established. Hongren saw this *gatha*
and realized that Huineng's state of enlightenment was
superior to that of Shenxiu and thereupon bestowed his
*kasaya* upon him. Huineng thus became the Sixth Patriarch.
His teachings of the Buddhist law were assembled by his
disciples into the *Platform Sutra*, one of the most important
classics of Zen Buddhism.

Our body is formed from the four elements of earth, water, fire and air and comprises the five attributes of sight, hearing, smell, speech, touch and thought. Where else can a real body be obtained? The mirror stand is also the product of various elements. Our mind is filled with fantasies that follow one upon another, appearing and disappearing, illusory and unreal. Where is something real to be found?

Our body and our thinking change all the time, our thoughts shift and flow and attain no end. This being so, how then can they attract any external dust?

Shenxiu's *gatha* teaches us how to apply ourselves to spiritual practice. Nevertheless, ridding oneself of filth and corruption through gradual cultivation is a seeking of the way, not enlightenment. Huineng's *gatha* by contrast, is the gateway to becoming a Buddha through an instant of enlightenment.

**Huineng**, 638–713, lost his father when a child. His family was poverty-stricken and he made a living from selling firewood. After leaving home he became a pupil of Zen Master Hongren, the Fifth Patriarch, and assumed his mantle becoming the Sixth Patriarch and founder of the Southern School of Zen.

# 9
## Buddha's Law Is of This World
### *Huineng*

*Buddha's law is of this world*
*And not beyond.*
*To search beyond*
*Seeks horns upon a rabbit.*

For many people, Buddhism is the early morning gong and evening drum of the ancient temple deep in the mountains, lamplight and yellowing scrolls, out of touch with our work and life. This is not the case. The Buddhist scriptures say that Buddhas are created upon earth not in heaven, so that spiritual practice and enlightenment are of this world too. If it leaves this world, Buddha's law becomes an edifice in space. Sakyamuni Buddha's teaching of the law for the world was designed to civilize and purify and to make a flawed and troubled world a Pure Land of perfect peace and tranquility.

Before Huineng, Chinese Zen emphasized the individual self-comprehension and experience of the practitioner in search of a state of emancipation completely different from the everyday world. The Southern School of Zen that followed Huineng concentrates upon how to attain the Buddhist truths in the current world and considers that methods such as the mere reliance upon study of the sutras and seated meditation cannot bring about true enlightenment. True enlightenment can only be experienced through daily life. Seeking so-called enlightenment beyond this world is fruitless. This idea became the basic tenet of Chinese Zen.

# 10

## Calling upon Master Rong at His Hut of Meditation
### *Meng Haoran*

*A monk's robe hangs in the hilltop hut,*
*Through the window, a water bird glides*
*In the unpeopled space beyond.*
*At dusk I took the downhill path,*
*And heard the sound of spring water,*
*Parting with regret.*

Inside the hut, a monk's robe hangs on the wall and outside the window, without a trace of humanity, water birds glide and hang in the air. The "hanging monk's robe" represents the monk's mood of detached leisure and the tranquility of the surroundings provide a backdrop to the monk's own elegance of temperament.

The robe is visible but not the person. What is Master Rong doing at this moment? Is he sipping tea with the visiting poet or practicing Zen in the depths of the mist? Or down the mountain enlightening the multitude of sentient beings?

As dusk approaches, the poet slowly follows the mountain path home. Amidst the beauty of the mountain path he unconsciously whiles away the half of dusk. As he descends, a mountain stream accompanies him, emitting a clear, tinkling sound, telling the blue hills of its regret and longing. The poet stops and looks back, his heart also surging with feelings of limitless yearning.

**Meng Haoran**, 689–740, famous poet of the height of the Tang dynasty. He spent most of his life as a hermit in the hills with other hermits, Buddhist monks and companions of the way for friends. Poetry as well-known as that of Wang Wei, known together as Wang Meng.

# 11
## A Hermit's Life in Zhongnan
*Wang Wei*

*In middle life I loved the way.*
*Now in age, retired beneath the southern hills,*
*When fancy strikes, I stroll alone,*
*Drunk with joy of sight and sound,*
*To water's head and seated watch the furling clouds,*
*And talk and laugh beyond the hour*
*With a forest ancient met by chance.*

The atmosphere of unhurried calm beneath the southern hills is utterly unlike that of the mundane world of dust. When fancy strikes is often the time when a person goes out alone and coming across something of great beauty becomes intoxicated with joy so that he does not feel alone at all. In search of tranquility he follows a stream to its source and watches the clouds at the edge of the sky billow and unfurl. These lines are full of the sense of Zen. The practice of Zen proceeds from existence towards emptiness, driving a boat against the current towards the source, against the flood of greed, anger, and delusion and back to the source of pure, unsullied human nature; then back again from the void to existence, to enjoy the clouds of the myriad worlds as they billow and disappear and the fish as they leap and the kites as they soar. Because this passage is so rich in the principles of Zen it was often quoted by historical Zen masters in their lectures.

When the time comes for the poet to return he meets, by chance, an old man with whom he laughs and chats with such enjoyment that he forgets the time. This passage has two moments of marvel. A chance meeting not sought or arranged, that follows the flow of cause: this is affinity. The other is "beyond the hour" caught in the moment and place to the point of forgetting to return: this is a sense of agreeable ease. Those who follow this sense are liberated and at ease, filled with the joy of the sense of Zen.

**Wang Wei**, 701?–761, style name Mojie (from *Weimojiejing*—the *Vimalakīrti-nirdeśa sūtra*). Took office under the banner of the An Lushan rebellion and was dismissed after it was put down. In his later years he lost his taste for official life and lived a hermetic life as a vegetarian Buddhist in a cottage in the Zhongnan hills, where he enjoyed the scenery and building his cottage at Wangchuan, and followed an existence of abstinence and Zen belief. This was not the impulse of a moment but the result of a longing for the path of enlightenment that had started in middle age. His works are exuberantly filled with the sense of Zen and samadhi—concentrated contemplation. Revered as the "Buddha of poetry".

# 12
## By Magnolia Wall
*Wang Wei*

*In the steep valley*
*The twig tip hibiscus flowers red*
*And by the mountain's lonely torrent,*
*One by one they bloom,*
*Then fall.*

There is a saying in Chinese "An orchid in an empty valley" used to describe the beauty of flowers as they blossom. The magnolia in the steep valley in this poem, like the orchid of the saying, possesses an essence of Buddhism that commands praise and respect.

The ancients said: "The absence of man does not prevent the orchid in the empty valley from flowering." Despite the absence of man to admire it, the magnolia that grows in a steep, remote valley will not refuse to emit the fragrance of life.

A man's many achievements in society are like the blossoming of a flower. It is of no importance whether or not people applaud. Confucius said: "Not to feel resentment when misunderstood is not that the act of a Gentleman?"

As in the prime of life the flower blossoms, and as at

the end of life the flower withers. Many people in the full flush of life become expansive and self-satisfied; at life's end they are eager for fame and reputation, unwilling to depart calmly, putting aside life and death, because their attachments are too strong. Every beginning has an ending and there is a fall to every rise. Flower calmly and wither tranquilly, without the arrogance of full bloom or the self-pity of withering away. Live with the splendor of the summer flower, die with the tranquility of the autumn leaf. The utmost of calm, of transcendence and of being at ease in oneself, that is the Buddhist essence of the magnolia.

You, who embody the spirit of all things, can you attain the state of the magnolia?

# 13

## A Reply to Sub-Treasurer Zhang

*Wang Wei*

*Now in age I love only solitude,*
*I have no heart for affairs of state.*
*Lacking grand designs and empty of wisdom,*
*I returned to the hills of old.*
*The wind in the pines blows aside my girdle*
*And the moon shines as I play the* qin.
*If you ask where lies the meaning in this,*
*I sing a fisherman's song*
*And row for the shore.*

In old age and following the ups and downs of an official career Wang Wei's only desire was for a quiet life. He had no interest in anything else.

He derides his own lack of talent and achievement in government and returns to the secluded forest hills that he knows so well. Nevertheless, there is a sense of unlimited responsibility in his derision. When he was an official he was required to attend court with his girdle neatly tied, but now free and easy in the forest with his girdle loose and blown aside by the wind in the pines, the freedom that he now feels is something that he could not have imagined in the past. As the moon shines down the poet plucks from the *qin* emotions and feelings of leisured seclusion and the beauty of the melody eases both heart and spirit. If you ask me about the meaning of life I start up a fisherman's song and row for the shore because I long ago put these sort of questions out of my mind. Answers that are not answers, bending in the wind and the beauty of the unhurried melody.

This kind of answer that is not an answer has all the poetic charm of the Zen "pointed phrases". Dongshan, a Zen master slightly later than Wang Wei, asked Master Yunyan: "May I seek instruction upon a question?" Master Yunyan replied: "I have an answer to all questions, but my answer is not to answer. You can ask me, but I cannot reply." "Since there are no questions that cannot be answered, why can there be no answer?" Yunyan replied: "That is because no answer is the only true answer!" (*The Compendium of Five Lamps*)

This poem expresses the joyful purity of spirit and heart and the unaffected sense of ease of the practitioner of Zen.

# 14
## Visiting the Incense Temple
*Wang Wei*


*I know not where the Incense Temple sits,*
*Yet climb the miles through clouded crags.*
*A path twists on beneath the trees,*
*But whence sounds the bell*
*In the mountain depths?*
*The spring water chokes amongst the rocks*
*And the sun shines cold on the pines.*
*Dusk falls by the empty pool*
*And Zen stills the dragons of desire.*


Not to know the location of the Incense Temple, and yet "unknowing" still to seek it, is a commonly occurring example of the Zen sensibility towards the pursuit of cause and affinity. By virtue of "not knowing" to enter the dense forest on a search and then miles later to arrive amongst mountain peaks wrapped in white cloud, vividly illustrates the utter seclusion of the Incense Temple, locked in mist and sealed in cloud.

In the dense forest, where the ancient trees reach to the heavens, there is no trace of man, just a moss covered path that twists onwards. The sound of a bell reverberates from somewhere, a steep valley deep in the hills, making the silence of the mountain forest quieter still.

The spring water streams through the sharp rocks with difficulty. It does not flow easily and seems to make a choking sound. In the thickly clustered trees in the depth of the mountains, there seems no warmth to the sun as its light falls on the pine forest. Rather, there is a sense of chill.

As the sun sets the poet arrives at the edge of a pool in the tranquil monastery and sits in silent meditation, conquering his internal desires. There is a Buddhist story of a pool in which a poisonous dragon lurks waiting to do harm. Using the limitless skill of the Buddhist law a monk elder overcomes the dragon and prevents it doing any further harm, a metaphor for overcoming the desires of the heart.

There is no direct description of the poet's visit to the Incense Temple. It is conveyed by oblique description of the surrounding scenery as a backdrop for the tranquil seclusion of the monastery. Finally, the act of meditation by the pool demonstrates the practice of Zen and illustrates the harvest reaped by visiting the temple.

## 15

# A Poem for the Zen Court behind the Poshan Temple
*Chang Jian*

*I enter the old temple at dawn*
*As the rising sun shines upon the lofty pines.*
*Through the bamboos a secluded path winds*
*To a Zen court in depths of flowers and trees.*
*The birds rejoice in the mountain air*
*And reflected pools cleanse the heart.*
*The hubbub of the world is hushed*
*But the bell's chime lingers on.*

This is the most famous of all temple poems (poems inscribed on the walls or otherwise left in temple premises by visiting poets). The quiet seclusion of the ancient temple set among the trees causes the poet a moment of instant admiration, and the rays of the rising sun stimulate a cheerful mood. Following a path set about with bamboos he arrives at the tranquil Zen court and discovers that it is really another world. The Zen court does not resemble the normal world with its cold, loneliness, drabness and depression, but is flourishing and full of vitality. See how magnificently the flowers blossom and how different they are from the shallow vulgarity of the world of dust and how they cause us to admire and linger in the intoxication of their beauty. The seclusion of the winding path is a quiet remoteness from the humdrum everyday; the "Zen court in depths of flowers and trees" represents a luxuriant sense of Zen. These two phrases appear like a ray of hope amongst the steep hills and turbulent waters, calling the Zen practitioner to transcend the mundane and to love the charm of life and to render it vividly.

The birds rejoice in the mountain air because they have found an ideal environment that suits their nature. The reflections from the clear water of the pools clears the heart of the impurities of the world of dust and washes it clean. This is an environment in which the spirit is consoled, purified and made joyful, leaving only the bright melody of the chiming bell as it draws us into a realm of tranquility and harmony where the mundane world is forgotten.

**Chang Jian**, 708–765?, poet of the mid-Tang. Dissatisfied with life as an official he spent a considerable time traveling to scenic spots and eventually took up life as a hermit in Hebei.

# 16

## The Sound of Chanting

### *Wei Yingwu*

*All creation sounds of itself*
*But space is still forever.*
*Sound springs from stillness*
*And to stillness returns.*

This poem uses the rise and fall of the sound of recitation to express the realization of the Zen theory of the impermanence and rise and fall of life.

All the "sounds" of life, such as fame, glory and reputation are formed from various causes and affinities. When you are at your most famous and most satisfied and prosperous, as if the sun were riding high in the sky, you can only avoid suffering through composure and the maintenance of an attitude of settled calm. When your reputation collapses and life is lonely and full of disappointment, as if the sun were sinking in the west, you can only avoid suffering through calm and by following the flow of cause and affinity and accepting fate.

The way has no form and there is no sound to noise. Zen allows us to see the formless and hear the soundless. That which is without form is the original form and that that has no sound is the original sound. Zen says that after

undertaking practice and cultivation a man may elevate his
mind to a state of harmony and tranquility:

Cloud, floating calmly in the sky;
Self, living calmly on earth.

Have you prepared yourself sufficiently to appreciate
the sound of tranquility?

**Wei Yingwu**, 737–791, poet of the mid-Tang. His poetry
has the natural simplicity of that of Tao Yuanming.

# 17

## A Reply to Prefect Wei Dan at the Donglin Temple
### *Lingche*

*In old age I take my ease and have no care*
*For the world outside,*
*Hempen garments and mats of straw suffice.*
*As to those who meet and say*
*How nice to give up office,*
*In the world of streams and woods,*
*Whoever met such a man?*

The Donglin Temple is a well-known monastery at Lushan Mountain. Wei Dan was the Prefect of Hongzhou (present-day Nanchang in Jiangxi province) and a fellow poet and convivial companion of Lingche. Wei Dan had sent a poem to Lingche expressing a wish to retire to the simple life. This poem is Lingche's reply that suggests that although Wei Dan thought of retiring as a hermit, this would never happen because he was incapable of genuine mental relaxation. He was merely paying lip service to the idea of withdrawal.

The Zen Master is at ease in his old age, unhurried and relaxed and pays no attention to anything apart from self-cultivation. He wears clothes made from hemp and sits on a straw mat, free and happy in himself.

Those dedicated to success in an official career talk of Zen with enthusiasm, of the charm of the secluded wooded heights and proclaim with every word the pleasures of giving up office. At best, these are mere words. There is not one of them who could really do it. From which can be seen how easy it is to talk of really casting away. Since it pointed out a universally existing fact, this well intentioned satire later became a neatly turned Zen phrase which ridiculed the pretensions of those who, unable to forget the mundane world, deliberately gave themselves airs and pretended to an extraordinary status.

The crux of Zen lies in the two words "cast away". Zen masters often use the phrase "See through, cast away, be at ease" to enlighten their pupils. If you cannot cast away, it is because you cannot see through. If you can see through, that is wisdom, to cast away is an achievement and being at ease is a convenience. When you can see through, then you can cast away. When you can cast away then you can be at ease.

**Lingche**, 746–816, left home to become a monk at an early age and became friends with Jiaoran and other well-known monks. During the reign of the Tang emperor Dezong visited Chang'an and became well known.

# 18

## To Zen Master Taoguang

*Bai Juyi*

*The single door that opens to the hills makes two,*
*Two temples were once the same.*
*From the east the streams run west to mingle*
*And from southern hills rise northern clouds.*
*Flowers bloom in front*
*But at rear are seen.*
*Bells above are heard below*
*And I think of my master's meditation place,*
*Where cassia flowers drift down one by one.*

The "single door that opens to the hills" of this poem refers to the hill gates of the lower and middle Tianzhu temples at Hangzhou. The two temples were originally one, beneath the northern peak of the Lingyin mountain. The eastern and western streams mingle and the clouds from the southern and northern hills become one. The flowers that bloom on the front terrace can be seen on the back terrace and the bell that sounds in the heavens can be heard by humanity and the world of dust. The poem uses the eight directions of North, South, East, West, front, rear, above and below to create a perfect realm of incomparable beauty and harmony. The final two lines imagine the beauty of the Zen master's place of meditation where the cassia flowers float down one by one from the palace of the moon. They also illustrate the elegant aesthetic of the master's Zen practice and the interaction between heaven and man to be found in its power of attraction.

As we recite and reflect we also become as one with it and are transformed into a rushing spring, a twist of white cloud, a thicket of wild flowers or the sound of a bell. In truth, when man interacts with man, with nature and with the Buddha-nature too and they become one, that is really when a perfect beauty is created in heaven and earth.

**Bai Juyi**, 772–846, style name Letian, known in later years by the title Hermit of Xiangshan. Poet and literary figure of considerable fame and extensive influence in the history of Chinese literature. The subjects of his poetry were wide-ranging, he wrote in many forms and the language was plain and easily understood. Works included Songs of Regret and Song of the Pipa Player.

# 19
## Peach Blossom at the Dalin Temple
*Bai Juyi*

*April in the land of man*
*And every flower has fallen,*
*But in the temple the peach tree blossoms still.*
*I sighed that spring had left no trace,*
*Not knowing that it lingered here.*

It was the first month of summer when the poet climbed the hill, just as spring was retreating and the blossom had fallen. But at this temple, set high in the hills, the season differed from that of the plains. At the Dalin temple the poet was met by the unexpected spring sight of a spread of just opened peach blossom in full flower. As he saw the sight before his eyes the poet was deeply moved. He had been depressed by the rapid disappearance of spring and had not realized that its full flowering had moved to the precincts of Buddha. When this unanticipated beauty burst forth before his eyes he could only feel joy and amazement.

The blossom of mankind is our fame, status and money that can wither and fall in the blink of an eye. The earthly scene can dissolve in a puff of wind. The blossoming of Zen however, transcends time and space, brilliant and vibrant forever. It is a life filled with spiritual enlightenment.

Today, countless people throughout the world may find that their spirit can be both fired by the wisdom of Zen and entrusted to it.

# 20

# An Inscription for the Monk's Quarters
## of the Helin Temple
*Li She*

*Mired in drunken dreams all day,*
*Of a sudden, I hear that spring is nearly done*
*And force myself up towards the hills.*
*By a bamboo court I meet a monk,*
*From whose lips I gain*
*The consolation of half a day.*

A man living in the red dust of the mundane, entangled in
humdrum tasks and befuddled with dreams is disinclined
even to recognize the presence of spring. Only when
he realizes that spring is almost done does he force his
reluctant body up into the hills for a walk. By chance he
comes across a remote and secluded bamboo courtyard
where, after he has talked to the monk a while, he gains
the great consolation of half a day's leisure.

As far as the ordinary, everyday person deeply
entangled in the mundane is concerned, a trip to the hills
is something that only happens occasionally. It is difficult
for someone mired in dreams all day to have any deep
exchange with a monk. Chatting is merely a diversion from
boredom. After this temporary respite of leisure he will

plunge back into the red dust, return to his original state and continue life as before. Despite this however, when somebody who is out of spirits visits a remote, elegant and secluded environment they can, through its influence, gain some rarely attainable joy for their numbed and blinded spirit. This is a well-known poem that embodies the remote leisure of the sense of Zen. The Helin temple is in Zhenjiang in Jiangsu province.

**Li She**, an official at the capital during the reign of the Tang emperor, Wenzong (806–840). Later resigned and wandered in the area of Guilin.

# 21
## An Occasional Poem
### *Pang Yun*

*There's nothing strange in mundane matters,*
*Harmony is the key.*
*No need for choice or gain and loss*
*But keep one's nature true.*
*Scarlet and purple differ but in name,*
*No dust stains the hills.*
*Enlightenment's mystic power*
*Is drawing water and hewing wood.*

The mundane matters of Zen are walking, dwelling, sitting, and sleeping. There is nothing extraordinary about them, except that one's own mind must be in harmony. There is no hankering after things in the great way, no aspirations. Enlightenment comes naturally and of itself.

There is no choice to be made amongst the myriad entities of the world, no sense of the difference between sacred or ordinary or concept of distinction between purity and impurity. Thus there can be no conflict with one's true nature.

In the world of appearance there is a distinction between scarlet and purple but who was it that conferred this difference upon them? It is merely a distinction in name, their original nature is void. In exactly the same way that the blue hills cannot be deceived by the world of dust so is the absolutely pure mind immune to the pollution of the dust of these names.

After enlightenment the mystic power of Zen lies in the very ordinary activities of drawing water and chopping firewood. It should not be thought that these mystic abilities are the sort of supernatural powers that involve a halo behind your head and clouds at your feet.

A disciple asked Zen Master Huihai: "Master, do you practice Zen diligently?" Master Huihai said: "I do." "What secret is there to it?" "Eating when hungry and sleeping when tired." The disciple said: "Everybody is like that, why is that not practice, yet what you do is practice?" The Master said: "It's not the same. When they eat, it is not eating but every variety of vain delusion; when they sleep it is not slumber but the planning of stratagem, so it cannot be practice. But when I eat as a Zen master it is merely eating, and sleeping is merely sleeping, and that is practice. If you can manage this, this is the greatest secret."

**Pang Yun**, mid-Tang hermit. Dates unknown. Detached, carefree and transcendental. Over the last 1,000 years has become a model followed by many Chinese scholar/ officials. Left nearly 200 *gatha* and poems. Able in argument, he expounded the essentials of Zen in the *gatha* style of the Buddhist sutras.

# 22

## An Occasional Poem
### *Pang Yun*

*Scholars arrive from everywhere,*
*Each to the study of the uncaused.*
*This is the place of Buddha choice,*
*Where only minds empty of dust succeed.*

The Tang dynasty Zen master, Danxia Tianran, was
originally a Confucian who had intended to go to Chang'an
to take the imperial examinations. On the way, somebody
said to him: "It is better to choose Buddha than an official
career." He then abandoned the idea of an official career
and chose to study Buddhism under Zen masters Mazu
and Shitou. Subsequently, the Zen halls of the Zen sect
became known as "places of Buddha choice", indicating
that Zen halls were special places where, through rigorous
cultivation and training in Zen, a practitioner could
achieve enlightenment and become a Buddha.

From ancient times, countless numbers of people have
not shrunk from hardship and have gathered in Zen halls
to cultivate the Zen practice of the uncaused[1]. Those who

---

[1] In Chinese *wuwei*, the Daoist theory of inaction, but in Buddhism
something that stands apart from cause and effect.

have succeeded have been those who have been able to empty their minds to accept purity.

This experience of the author Pang Yun is heartfelt. On the point of death a friend said to him: "You are about to leave us, please give us some words of instruction." He replied: "Discard those delusions of distinction and attachment that you have for the wisdom and mercy that you have not." Having said this he died with his head pillowed on his friend's knee.

All the afflictions of life are due to the unceasing accumulation of desires. We unendingly seek outside our self in an attempt to bolster ourselves with things that are fundamentally useless. We are unaware of the delusions and distinctions that we harbor and are unwilling to discard greed, anger, and ignorance. If we are able to empty our minds, then all will be complete and we can become a Buddha.

Because of the influence of this poem, tablets inscribed "Only minds empty of dust succeed" still hang in the Zen hall of many monasteries. It is a matter of regret that though practitioners abound like carp in a river, those who succeed are as rare as the feathers of a phoenix or the horn of a unicorn.

# 23
## A *Gatha* of the Law
### *Longshan*

*In three huts have I dwelt this life,*
*But one mystic light has shone*
*To create a myriad leisured states.*
*Do not test me with tales of right and wrong,*
*I have no truck with the floating life*
*Of forced fact and this and that.*

One day, the Zen Master Dongshan passed through
Longshan and saw a vegetable leaf floating in a mountain
stream. Parting the undergrowth he followed upstream
and came across Longshan, a monk of lean and disheveled
appearance living in a straw hut, and the two thereupon
had an exchange of witticisms. After Dongshan had bid
farewell, Longshan recited this *gatha*, set fire to his hut and
disappeared into the hills. No one knew what became of
him. This *gatha* describes the Zen sense of enlightenment
that transcends the material.

In this world there is no need for luxurious
accommodation, clothing or food. However vast your
house you will only require so much space for sleeping,
however extensive your landholdings there are only three
meals in a day. As long as your mind is calm, a simple hut

can be the finest accommodation. At the same time, as long as the mind is illuminated with the mystic light of wisdom, whatever the environment, there is nowhere where you cannot be at ease. In these states, do not argue with me on the basis of worldly right and wrong, gain and loss because I put the mundane concepts of right and wrong in the world of dust out of my mind long ago.

The head of the ordinary person, blind to the mystic light, spins at these myriad states, fraught in mind and condition. Bathed in the mystic light the practitioner of Zen is not confused by the condition but uses his mind to control it and naturally creates the myriad states of leisure.

Man often suffers the torments of affliction. However when this mystic light in your life is lit, the seething chaos of the present will be transformed into a Pure Land.

**Longshan**, pupil of the well known Tang dynasty Zen master Mazu Daoyi, lived as a hermit for the whole of his life and never entered the mundane world.

# 24
## A Trip South of the City
### *Han Yu*

*Those who scramble after fame,*
*Gain not the ease of half a day.*
*Without a companion I come*
*And toast the southern hills alone.*

Short though it is, this poem is dense with implication,
profound and thought provoking. It seems to come from
the same stable as Bai Juyi's poem *Crossing the Avenue of the
Gate of Heaven*:

> "The snow has gone,
> And in the south spring has come.
> Hills of distant blue face the reddened dust,
> A thousand chariots, ten thousand horses
> Throng every street.
> But none turn their head to see the hills."

Sima Qian said with regret in the *Record of History*:
"When all under heaven prospers, they come for gain;
when all under heaven is in chaos they leave for gain." Put
into the language of Zen: "Losing self, one pursues the
material; in pursuit of the material one loses self." Having

lost one's true nature one takes to the pursuit of external material things; the pursuit of the material then brings further loss of one's true nature. But mutual contact and knowledge of hills and water and of nature points out a road home for mankind. In his well-known poem, *Stone on the Mountain*, Han Yu said in effect: "What a pity, why is it that those friends of mine are still caught up in the red dust into their old age, and do not know the blue hills and the clear water that can lead them back to their true nature?"

In truth, where there is the Zen spirit to look at the hills, there is also the knowledge and ease of Zen.

**Han Yu**, 768–824, style name Tuizhi, praised by Ming writers as the greatest of the eight great poets of the Tang and Song dynasties, also known as "Master of the Written Word", "Literary Model of a Hundred Generations". His self-appointed task was the revival of Confucianism. He was an opponent of Buddhism early in his life and was demoted and exiled to Chaozhou for having presented a petition criticizing it. Later, through association with Buddhist monks his attitude softened and he had an inclination to Zen and returned to his self-nature.

## 25

# For Elder Monk Weiyan of Yaoshan

*Li Ao*

*Body forged to the form of a crane*
*Standing beneath the ancient pines,*
*Two sutras by his side.*
*I ask the master to show the way,*
*Without a word, he points to the clouds in the sky*
*And the water in the vase.*

Li Ao visited Master Weiyan in Yaoshan mountain and found him reading sutras by the window. He did not rise nor look up and greet him. Irritated, Li Ao said: "To have heard of one's fame is superior to mere sight!" The Zen Master said: "Why does the Governor favor his ears over his eyes?" Li Ao quickly saluted and apologized and then asked: "What is Zen?" The Zen Master pointed to the sky and then to the ground. Li Ao failed to understand and the master said: "The clouds are in the sky and the water is in the vase." Li Ao was enlightened with joy and immediately recited this verse.

The feeling that is inspired by the sight of a crane is one of elegance and nobility. In appearance the Zen Master Weiyan was thin, in spirit awe inspiring. He had very much the air and style of one who has found the way, a sight to inspire joy and peace of mind and completely different from the crude, ordinary monks. The poet is able to praise the Zen Master's internal sense of cultivation on the basis of his refined external appearance.

The ancient pines demonstrate the secluded beauty of the Zen Master's surroundings. The pine trees grow in tranquil profusion, a suitable place for Zen enlightenment. Cranes like to nest in pine trees most of all and the presence of the Zen Master beneath naturally draws people to think of the sacred cranes as well. The mention of two sutras indicates that they have not yet been opened and are still in their cases. Why? Because when Zen Master Weiyan speaks of reading the sutras he means nothing more than "only using the sutras to protect my eyes from the light, not for reading" demonstrating the Zen master's state of true liberated detachment, a style that can only be attained by those of extraordinary enlightenment, so different from those with their heads buried in the sutras. This poem reveals the Zen Master's deep knowledge of the scriptures and that he did not stoop to inflating his reputation through study of the sutras. His perception was filled with self-confidence.

Zen Master Weiyan had not publicly expounded the law for some time and disciples were eager to hear him lecture. He therefore ordered someone to sound the bell and when all had gathered together left the hall without a word. A disciple asked him the reason and he said: "There are teachers who teach the scriptures, there are teachers who teach the law, I am a Zen master and how can Zen be taught?" It can be seen that Weiyan's employment of the device of "without a word" was because of his wish not to use words to describe Zen. Moreover, "without a word" was not entirely out of a basic unwillingness to speak, since the student was there waiting for instruction. But, how was the Zen master to instruct him?

"The clouds in the sky / And the water in the vase." This is the "way" that the Zen master indicated and that Li Ao comprehended. The clouds in the sky turn from wind to nothing, billowing at will; the water in the vase is still and serene, its clarity perceptible. If you are a cloud then you act as a cloud floating free in the sky; if you are water then you act as water, at ease in the vase. No matter what environment a person may be in, he must always grasp the moment and not indulge in profitless speculation about this and that, otherwise he will fail to gain what he sought and lose the joy of the moment. The clouds are just clouds unrestrained and at ease; the water is just water still and at ease. Grasping one's environment, and living the moment is the real essence of Zen.

**Li Ao**, 772–836, style name Xizhi, Tang dynasty literary figure and philosopher. Whilst prefect of Langzhou he frequently visited Zen Master Weiyan the abbot of Yaoshan. Subsequently wrote *A Return to One's Nature* and combined the principles of Zen with the theories of Confucianism, heralding the neo-Confucian rationalist School of Principle of the Song to Ming dynasties.

# 26

## Escape the Toils of the World
### *Xiyun*

*To escape the toils of this world of dust*
*Grasp the halter and strive beyond the day-to-day.*
*Without the cold that cuts the bone,*
*No scent from the blossoming plum*
*Ever greets the nostrils.*

In Zen, enlightenment is not achieved lightly. Avoiding
the suffering of the toils of the world of dust and entering
the luminous world of the state of Zen is no idle matter.
Overcoming delusions and distractions is like grasping
the halter of a stubborn ox. You cannot relax your grip
for a moment. Results come only from unremitting and
painstaking effort. Only the "cold that cuts the bone" can
produce the "scent from the blossoming plum", thus it can
be seen how very difficult it is to achieve enlightenment.

The practice of Zen is like rowing a boat against the
current upstream towards the source. In the rapid current
of the habits of greed, anger and ignorance, going against
the flow, where if you do not advance you recede, is an
achievement of the utmost difficulty without great courage
and perseverance. In the practice of Zen, "the familiar
becomes strange and the strange becomes familiar" and

"the difficult to relinquish is easily relinquished and the difficult to do can be done." The denseness of the causes of the world of dust, the complications of secular affairs and the various kinds of fame and fortune all obscure our minds. To rid ourselves of these causes and escape the toils of the world we must rein in our natural impulses.

In the poem the bitter cold experienced by the plum enhances its fragrance and is used as a metaphor for the arduous practice that leads to a perfect result. Philosophically apt and vivid, the poem is well-known and still has popular appeal today.

**Xiyun**, ?–850, left home when young to become a Buddhist at Huangbo Hill in Fuzhou. Visited Zen Master Huaihai in Jiangxi and studied with him. Preached Buddhism at the Da'an Temple in Hongzhou (present-day Jiangxi province). Monks flocked to hear him and Zen Master Yixuan, the founder of the Linji (Rinzai) school of Zen became one of his disciples. Because of his passion for the hills he was known as Huangbo and was later called Zen Master Huangbo.

# 27

## Unwilling to Leave through An Empty Door
### *Shenzan*

*Unwilling to leave through an empty door,*
*Caught in ignorance against the paper window pane.*
*A century burrowing in ancient script,*
*When at last shall I emerge?*


After Shenzan had received instruction in the Buddhist
law from Zen Master Huaihai, he returned to the Dazhong
temple. His teacher was reading the sutras beside a
window and it so happened that a bee was buzzing against
the window paper in an attempt to get out. On seeing
this Shenzan said: "The world is so vast but yet this bee's
unwilling to go free; buried in paper as it is, the day
that it can escape will never come." Shenzan thereupon
recited this *gatha*. His teacher experienced a sudden flash
of enlightenment, called everybody together, and asked
Shenzan to preach to them.

The "empty door" of the poem is actually a wide open
door, the opposite of the paper window and is a metaphor
for the doorway of Buddha and of Zen enlightenment.
"Ancient script" is old paper with the superficial meaning
of window paper but the actual sense of the Buddhist
sutras and ancient texts.

When the Sakyamuni Buddha held the flower at the meeting at Mount Lingshan and Mahakasyapa smiled, in that moment, Zen was poetically transmitted from the mind of Sakyamuni to that of Mahakasyapa without a word being spoken. Zen is an immediate vital living experience, which, were it to inhabit language, concepts, logic or names and appearances, would be just window paper. Even a lifetime spent boring away would not secure release and you would never obtain spiritual freedom.

Zen requires no language. How can you achieve a life of enlightenment buried in a pile of old paper?

Each one of us possesses a spiritual doorway and yet most of us insist upon burrowing in piles of old paper. The result is a weariness of body and soul, fatigue of mind and ever receding aspirations. Where is the opportunity of enlightenment to be found in that?

**Shenzan**, Tang dynasty Zen master. Studied at the Dazhong temple in Fuzhou and subsequently travelled on foot to meet Zen Master Huaihai who transmitted his wisdom to him. In order to repay their kindness, Shenzan returned to the Dazhong temple and preached there.

# 28

# Untitled

*Liangjia*

*Search not elsewhere,*
*It is too far from self.*
*Look on one's own*
*And it is everywhere.*
*It is I but I am not it,*
*This is the way to truth.*

The Zen Master Dongshan was crossing a river by boat one
day when he saw his reflection in the water and composed
this poem in a moment of sudden enlightenment. The
reflection represented the actual self, whilst the physical
body represented the self of appearance. The actual self
could not leave the self of appearance on a quest of its
own.

The quest for the enlightenment of the true self has
to proceed from within and cannot possibly be sought of
others. If one does not seek within oneself but seeks it of
others, the result is an ever-increasing distance from the
real self.

It is precisely because of the ability to undertake
the quest for the real self on one's own that its original
appearance can be found everywhere.

The real self, the true nature, is a state attained through cultivation to the utmost, although it encompasses self, "self" is still burdened with form, still encumbered with the day-to-day and still some distance from the real self and far from on equal terms with it.

Everything must be understood in this sense before there can be any accord with the true self and original nature.

**Liangjia**, 807–869, Tang dynasty founder of the Caodong School of Zen, a late Tang master of the Zen School. He taught Zen at Dongshan in Jiangxi province while his disciple Benji taught at Caoshan, hence the name Caodong School.

# 29

## The Story of the Fishing Boat
### *Decheng*

*The fishing line plunges deep,*
*And ten thousand ripples follow upon the one.*
*In the chill water at quiet of night,*
*No fish seize the bait*
*But the boat rows home*
*Loaded with the gleaming moon.*

A mood of quiet elegance pervades this popular poem of Zen analogy. A small boat bearing a relaxed fisherman floats tranquilly on the green, mirror-like surface of the river. He drops a long fishing line into the depths. But he has something other than fishing on his mind. He appears to fish but in fact he seeks the way and for a disciple who will succeed to his Zen style.

There is no need to dwell on the fact that the practitioner of Zen constantly seeks the way and that the act of fishing is a metaphor for this. However, why is it that this verse also borrows the fishing metaphor to represent the search for a disciple? It is because it is one verse of a number under the same title. The other verses make it quite clear that fishing is also a metaphor for the search for a disciple.

The instant that the hook is thrown into the water
it causes a ripple. Thereafter thousands of ripples spread
from its center. Everything in the cosmos is one entity.
The birth of one cause leads to the birth of a myriad other
causes.

The night is tranquil and the water cold and the fish
will not take the bait. It is easy to see that the search for
the way has always been difficult and disciples hard to find.

Although the fish do not take the bait, though the way
is difficult to find and a disciple hard to come by, it is of no
consequence. It is enough to concentrate upon and enjoy
the process. The fisherman is intoxicated by the delicate
clarity of nature and he brims with emotion, contentedly
rowing home a boat loaded full of the gleaming moon.
His destination is the home village of tranquil spiritual joy
where water and sky are one. But in fact he has already
arrived home, even as he makes his way there.

The poem uses the metaphor of the fishing line to
represent the search for the way and for a disciple. In the
metaphor, as the quest for the way and the search for a
disciple continues, the way remains profoundly hidden
and the affinity with the disciple still distant. As the ripples
spread both quests have to wait upon the ripening of the
affinity and cannot be forced. The fish not taking the bait
represents the difficulty of seeking one's original nature
and of finding a disciple. The boat loaded with the moon
metaphorically represents the bright purity of the way
and the imprinting of minds that spontaneously occurs
between master and disciple. The Zen master casts his

hook not for fish but to follow affinity and destiny, to live in the present and to enjoy the delights of the spirit.

To live calmly in the present is to regard the "journey itself as home" and to embody one's whole sense of purpose in the processes of the present to the extent that the final aim no longer appears important. Just as Wang Ziyou of the Jin dynasty rose in the middle of a snowy night and took a boat to visit his old friend Dai Kui and then turned back on reaching his friend's door after an overnight journey, remarking when asked why: "I came on an impulse and now that it is exhausted why should I visit Dai?"

This poem also contains much of the Zen sense of "Strive in the cause but leave the effect to destiny". In cause he came, fished and tried hard. In effect, the water was cold and the fish did not bite, the quest for the way was difficult and a disciple hard to find. He calmly accepted this consequence and ceased to worry, following, instead, the flow of cause and effect and rowing the boat of the spirit home loaded with the gleaming moon. This mentality and type of conduct are themselves both an important achievement and a joy.

**Decheng**, 820–858, a Zen pupil of Master Weiyan of Yaoshan. A hermit on the banks of the river Wu in Huating who preached by boat, hence his title, the Boat Monk.

# 30

# A *Gatha* on the Proclamation Returning Monks
# to the Secular World
### *Zhizhen*

*The moon shines upon us all,*
*How can wearing the white of the common world*
*Degrade those who perceive the void?*
*Who can say that living thus obstructs the way?*
*I take the hermit Weimo as my guide.*

When the Tang emperor Wuzong (814–846) suppressed
Buddhism in 845, Zen Master Zhizhen was forced
to return to the secular world. Although garbed as a
commoner his Buddhist beliefs remained strong. The
theme of the poem is that a return to the secular world
does not prevent the practice of the way. The moon in
the sky shines brightly everywhere. The fact that one may
have changed one's garb is no obstacle to the practice of
Buddhism and will not adversely affect achievement. The
genuine follower of the way is not influenced by whether
he practices in a monastery or in the world. Provided
one is resolute in the way, it is equally possible to achieve
enlightenment and become a Buddha in an ordinary
household. The Sixth Patriarch said: "In the matter of
practice, it may be undertaken at home and not necessarily

in a monastery." In Buddhism Weimojie is regarded as a
reincarnation of Vimalakirti. Weimojie achieved Buddha-
hood as a lay practitioner (hence, not in a monastery) so a
return to the secular world should not be regarded as an
obstacle to the practice of the way. Practicing the way as a
commoner can just as well lead to great achievement.

The true Zen monk will maintain his resolution in
the way and reach the proper fruits of practice under any
circumstances.

**Zhizhen**, 781–865, disciple of Ma Zu's disciple Huaihui
of the Zhangjing Temple who lived at Guishan in Fuzhou.
"Ignore the texts, admire the Zen."

# 31

# A Summer Poem for the Zen Hall of Master Wukong

*Du Xunhe*

> *Three scorching summer days,*
> *Cassock clad behind closed doors*
> *Without the shade of pine or bamboo.*
> *Zen has no need for cool hills or water,*
> *Quench the fires of notion within,*
> *And you will be cool enough.*

This poem uses vivid imagery to portray the Zen truth of the natural coolness and calm of the spirit. The three scorching summer days are the hottest days of the year. The Zen master, clad in a *kasaya* sits meditating in the Zen hall with no concessions because of the heat. What are the conditions under which the Zen master meditates? He is completely exposed to the broiling heat of the sun without the shade of pines or bamboos to provide protection from the sun for the roof of the hall. Had it been any ordinary person they would long ago have become uncomfortable at sitting erect. That the Zen master could sit unperturbed in meditation in this furnace, what level of detachment, calm and ease does that represent!

Clearly there is no requirement for the cool of

water and hills for successful meditation. The Zen
practitioner need not blindly emphasize the conditions
and environment of the external world. He needs only
to stamp out the fires of notion in his heart, to have no
distractions or delusions and even in the most torrid heat
to be at peace with himself, so that he can still feel as if he
is immersed in a world of coolness.

Quenching the fires of notion means eliminating
the concept of opposites from the mind: rich and poor,
noble and base, many and few, hot and cold. Once the
concept of opposites has been banished, the present then
consists of transparent coolness. The fires are the fires
of the afflictions of the mundane world. Escaping from
them does not really solve the problem, only by delving
into affliction can we demonstrate an understanding of it.
Joy and suffering are psychological phenomena, once the
opposition between joy and suffering is dissolved there will
be psychological harmony.

Bai Juyi's poem *A Poem in the Heat for the Zen Hall of
Master Hengji* has the same meaning:

"All madly flee the summer heat,
The Zen master alone stays within.
But in the hall there is no heat
For if the mind is calm, the body is cool."

The lines "Zen has no need for cool hills or water, /
Quench the fires of notion within, / And you will be
cool enough" subsequently became a widely circulated

Zen saying, used by many masters to enlighten their pupils. In a *koan* to be found in the *Record of the Blue Rock* (known as "the first book of Zen") somebody asked Zen Master Dongshan: "How should one escape the heat of summer and the cold of winter?" Dongshan replied: "Go somewhere where there is neither heat nor cold." The questioner asked further: "Where is there neither heat nor cold?" Dongshan replied: "Cold and the cold will kill you, hot and the heat will kill you!" The questioner still failed to understand and asked Zen Master Huanglong: "What should I do?" Zen Master Huanglong cracked the puzzle in a phrase: "Zen has no need for cool hills or water, / Quench the fires of notion within, / And you will be cool enough." Nature changes from summer heat to winter cold and the life of man contains both dark and light, perfection and imperfection; it has always been difficult to make a complete whole of this. The Zen attitude is that one should not avoid it but look inside the question and become one with it for living proof of affliction and enlightenment.

There have been Zen masters who have given their lives for these three lines.

In 16th century Japan, after destroying the forces of his opponent Takeda Shingen, Oda Nobunaga, out of respect for Takeda's teacher Kaizen, visited the Erin monastery bearing gifts and invited Kaizen to appear. Kaizen, however, paid not the least attention. This was a great blow to Oda's self-esteem. Following receipt of information that the monastery had concealed and protected Takeda's retainers and had covered up their escape, Oda ordered his troops to set the monastery on fire. Kaizen, after calmly reciting the three lines "Zen has no need for cool hills or water, / Quench the fires of notion within, / And you will be cool enough" plunged himself into the fire and entered the ultimate realm of coolness.

**Du Xunhe**, 846–904, late Tang poet. Heir to the realism of Du Fu and Bai Juyi, his poems reflected the darkness of late Tang society and the suffering of the people. Their language is simple and easily understood.

# Five Dynasties
## (907–960)

# 32

# My Home's in the Min Hills

*Huaijun*

*My home's in the Min hills, east more east,*
*Where flowers flower red, year on year.*
*Now back in the place where red flowers were,*
*I see flowers flowering red once more.*


This richly expressive poem is one of the jewels of Zen poetry. In Zen "Returning home and settling down" is a metaphor for sudden enlightenment and clearing the mind to see one's nature. Here, "home" is the home of the spirit. "East more east" suggests that it is at a considerable distance. In fact, it is not far away at all, it is always there waiting for you to return. The reason we feel it is so far away, is that we have wandered for too long, moving further and further away from our spiritual home.

The pure Buddha spirit resembles the scenery of our home village, gorgeous yet warm and fragrantly inviting. Before we lost our original nature and wandered to the edge of the world, this scenery was imprinted deep in our minds, insistently calling upon the prodigal son to return at every waking moment.

I have ended my spiritual wandering, achieved enlightenment and returned to my spiritual home, where, once more, I have seen the glory of the Buddha-nature, like a flower in full bloom.

Like a flower that never wilts, the Buddha spirit has neither birth nor extinction. It is our form that weakens and our spirit that suffers. After an encounter with the pain of wandering we are joyfully surprised to discover that there is a state of neither birth nor extinction where the distinctions of life and death do not exist. Once the fires of desire are extinguished, the mind achieves a mood of peace and tranquillity.

With its resemblance to the repetitive chanting of a children's song and its core image of red flowers the poem produces a strong and vivid impression and has a soul stirring sense of beauty.

Whether you return or not, the flowers will be there in the same place still as red as ever.

Do not take the road of no return in search of desire. Man's greatest reward is to turn homewards early.

**Huaijun**, monk of the late Tang-early Five Dynasties. A fine poet. Aloof and highly principled.

# 33

## A *Gatha* for the Enlightenment of Monks
### *Jingcen*

*At the pole top an acrobat sits stock still,*
*His skill yet far from truth.*
*At the pole top he must exercise more,*
*To be one with the myriad worlds.*

The ability to stand or sit motionless at the top of a
hundred foot pole is a highly developed acrobatic skill
achieved through long and rigorous training. To achieve the
hundred foot pole of cultivation is a great enlightenment,
but one cannot stop there. Pausing by oneself at an
advanced level of enlightenment is not thorough
enlightenment. There must be progress from the top of the
pole. One must leap forward from this enlightenment and
then become one with the myriad worlds, changing from
seeking enlightenment above to transforming all sentient
beings below, returning to the real world and grimy faced
at the cross roads, to bring deliverance to all sentient
beings. This is the only true way of becoming one with the
myriad worlds (the realm of utmost beauty, virtue and
attainment), so that they then become the greatest hope of
our lives.

Practitioners of Zen often say: "Sakyamuni and

Dharma are still in the process of cultivation" and "The road up is also the road down." All those who study seek enlightenment, but enlightenment is in no way the ultimate destination but a new beginning. The real value of the life of the Zen practitioner lies in turning aside from the realm of personal enlightenment and mingling in the market place of the world.

The Zen Master Weishan proclaimed that after death he would become the bullock for a lay family and this Mahayana mood of compassion for others in the sense of "All may become a Buddha or an ancestor, but only Weishan became a water buffalo" inspired the progress of countless practitioners of Zen.

**Jingcen**, monk of the late Tang-early Five Dynasties. Studied under Master Puyuan of Nanquan. He lived at the Luyuan Temple in Changsha where he taught Zen and was known as the monk of Changsha. Skilled in repartee and debate.

# 34

# A *Gatha* upon Enlightenment after Viewing Peach Blossom

## *Zhiqin*

> *For thirty hard years I've sought the way,*
> *Through leaf fall and blossom.*
> *But now I've seen the peach tree bloom,*
> *I do not doubt at all.*

This well-known poem of enlightenment describes the search for enlightenment and the joy that follows attainment. For thirty years spring and autumn change, the flowers blossom and wither, the search for enlightenment is endless.

After lengthy self-cultivation and a search for the way the author finally achieves true enlightenment only after viewing the peach tree in bloom and no longer has any doubts about his own feelings.

What enlightenment is it that gives him such self-confidence? Could it be that the blossoming and withering of the peach tree represents the impermanence and reincarnation that is the lot of all sentient beings? Is the luxuriance of the peach blossom a metaphor for the fact that everything arises from a combination of cause and effect? Does the blossoming of the peach tree suggest that enlightenment comes with the fullness of ability? Does the splendor of the blossom suggest that the world of color[1] manifests the original world? For a thousand years there have been differing views as to the essential meaning of the author's enlightenment. Perhaps each view strikes home the essential truth of a particular aspect or perhaps every view is so much hot air.

In fact, whatever the nature of the author's enlightenment, it is of little importance. Each person has their own individual perception of the way. The attraction of this poem lies in the fact that unremitting perseverance over 30 years, in order to achieve enlightenment, earns our respect; and secondly, that the confidence in enlightenment, the absolute lack of doubt and boldness of vision in its attainment is a matter for admiration.

**Zhiqin**, late Tang-early Five Dynasties monk. Known as the monk of Lingyun because he lived at the Lingyun Temple in Fuzhou. He left only this single poem.

---

[1] *Sejie*, the world of color, one of the three worlds of Buddhism, above the world of desire but below the world without color (*wusejie*).

# 35

# Sitting in Meditation on the South Terrace
*Shou'an*

*Above an incense burner on the south terrace,*
*Sitting in still meditation the day long,*
*All care forgotten.*
*Delusions depart un-banished.*
*And I am free from distraction.*

This poem describes the process of ridding oneself
of all anxiety and coming to an understanding of the
undistracted state of Zen calm.

Seated in meditation on the south terrace while
burning incense, the mind is tranquil and the heart full of
joy. In a state of Zen calm there is no sense of time and the
whole day passes imperceptibly. The notions of right and
wrong, present and void, rich and poor, noble and base,
bodhi and affliction, Buddhas and demons, existence and
*nirvana* have all been swept away but a sense of distinctions
remains. Those who lack spiritual power would be unable
to sustain control of their own notions for a single minute,
let alone a day.

An ordinary person encounters many delusions while
meditating and suppresses them through devices such
as deep breathing and reciting the names of the Buddha

or mantras. However, the Zen master has no need to deliberately eradicate delusion, no need to force the mind free from chaos or suppress its agitation because he has, through cultivation, already reached an elevated state, where there are no delusions to be found and where the mind has the clarity of still water, a state of profound spiritual skill.

The Tang dynasty Zen master Shiyan used to meditate seated on a rock and often conversed with himself in a monologue.

"Master!" he called to self.
"Uh!" self replied.
"Do not be deluded!"
"Quite right, quite right!" said self.
"Don't be hoodwinked by others!"
"Of course not, of course not!" replied self.

This is a highly skilled technique. Moreover, the poem displays the state attained through a perfected technique whose self-confidence and detachment can be found in Li Dong's *Poem for a Monk:*

"Sitting at leisure upon a rock
And gazing at the water's flow,
Wanting to wash my Zen robe
But there is no dust to wash."

As well as Zhizen's *Gatha:*

"Since in nature there was no dust,
Why need to cleanse?
If the body is sound,
Why seek a cure?"

It is also found in the Sixth Patriarch, Huineng's penetrating pronouncement:

"The beginning had no substance,
Where then was the dust?"

**Shou'an**, senior monk of the Five Dynasties, details of life unknown.

# 36

## Planting Rice
### *Qici*

*Head down I plant each fist of seedling rice*
*And glimpse the water mirrored sky.*
*Six pure roots and rice will sprout,*
*As I step back towards the front.*

This poem uses the metaphor of the peasant planting rice to convey a sense of the philosophy of life. Rice is planted whilst stepping backwards so as not to trample on the freshly planted seedlings and also to keep them in neat lines. Thus, whilst one is withdrawing or stepping backwards the actual planting is moving forward towards completion step by step, so that in actual fact withdrawal is progress. In this case, the metaphor is extremely obvious. The ancients said "to go back is to proceed" and "nothing is as good as to step back". If we can take a step back in life, we can see that the world displayed before us is one of vast expanse. This is the action of the peasant planting handfuls of rice seedlings in the paddy fields.

The second line indicates that even in the most humble circumstances one can discover that one's pure spirit is like clear water and capable of holding a reflection of the world and everything in it.

The third line refers to the six roots or organs, eyes, ears, nose, tongue, body and sense which can only achieve the way if unpolluted by the dust of the mundane.

**Qici**, ?–916, Five Dynasties-Liang dynasty monk. He often carried a cloth bag suspended from a stick over his shoulder and was consequently known as the bag monk (*budai heshang*). He was able to predict both disaster and happiness. Later generations regarded him as a reincarnation of the Boddhisattva Maitreya.

# 37
## The Tree Before the Gate
*Judun*

*There is a tree before the gate*
*Where birds nest and fly,*
*Unbidden and unmissed.*
*To have a heart like that tree,*
*Would not offend the way.*

The metaphor of this poem is inspired by the scene before the eyes. The tree represents the practitioner's nature and mind and the attitude of the tree towards the birds represents the relationship between the practitioner's internal state of mind and the external environment, vivid in image and profound in its implications.

The tree is not conscious of or engaged with the birds. If they come, they come, if they go, they go. They were not invited to come and when they go, there is no intention to keep them or longing for them to return. This is the profoundest state of "receptivity".

If a person's Zen practice and attitude to universal phenomena can be like that of the tree, then it has reached a point of refinement and is in accord with the way, since it embodies the attitude of the way towards all phenomena.

The *Vegetable Roots Discourse* of the Ming dynasty says

that the mind resembles a bamboo forest or water in a pool and that external events are like the wind that blows over the forest or the goose that flies across the pool. When an event occurs the mind responds naturally. Once it is over it returns to its original state of tranquility. What degree of tranquility and vivacity is represented by such a mind? It embodies the essence of the saying from the *Diamond Sutra*: "Create the will not to dwell in temptation."

**Judun**, 835–923, left his family at the age of fourteen to become a monk and subsequently achieved enlightenment with Zen master Dongshan. He lived at Longyashan Mountain in Tanzhou (present-day Changsha in Hunan province) where he was known as the monk of Longya.

# 38
## To Those Who Chant
### *Judun*

*Buddhas are few but many chant the prayers.*
*Through long years of chanting,*
*They fall to the demon fire.*
*You may wish to become a Buddha,*
*But few have the undistracted mind.*

In Chinese Buddhism, the chanting of the Buddhist doctrine advocated by the Pure Land sect is a method of practice undertaken by many believers. Those who chant outnumber those who practice Zen. For the majority of believers, it saves trouble and is more convenient to chant or recite "Amitabha Buddha", enough to achieve paradise and sufficient to satisfy the mind without seeking to become a Buddha through the Buddha-self. This is why those who chant form the majority and few become a Buddha. Beyond this, what is more to be feared is the fact that chanting over time, contrariwise, makes it easy to become a demon.

Since the recitation of prayers depends mainly upon the power of the non-self, it requires the assistance of the power of the Bodhisattva to achieve life in the Pure Land. By contrast, Zen emphasizes the power of self, becoming a Buddha through self-cultivation and reliance upon one's own efforts.

The point of this poem lies in its last two lines: that the chanting of prayers requires a pure mind in order to achieve a state of non-distraction and near Buddha-hood. "Non-distraction" is not an inanimate state of non-distraction, without concept or thought but a properly integrated state of mind where distractions do not arise, a territory of cultivation that is extremely difficult to reach. Why is it that those who have spent a lifetime in Buddhist prayer and chanting have never become Buddhas? They go to the temple to chant every day but give up nothing, neither right and wrong, nor self and other, neither fame and profit nor the five desires (wealth, sex, fame, eating and sleeping) and six dusts (form, sound, fragrance, taste, touch and imagination), neither greed nor ignorance. Under these circumstances, ten lifetimes of prayer with such a disordered mind, let alone a single lifetime, could not achieve success.

Only prayer and chanting with an undistracted and integrated mind will bring you across the river of life and death and affliction to the shore of the Pure Land.

## 39

## A *Gatha* of the Mind's Enlightenment
### *Huileng*

*The way is embodied in all*
*But only man's will brings it close.*
*Sought in confusion in the past,*
*Now found like ice within a fire.*

This poem describes the tortuous search for one's original mind, the Buddha-nature and ultimate enlightenment. The presence of the way is manifested in the cycle of reincarnation and in the mortality of mankind. It is the true embodiment of the way that rules and controls everything within the universe. However, although the way is always apparent it has to be experienced personally before one can be indissolubly linked with it. Nevertheless, the way is not everything within the universe itself. If you equate everything with the way, then the difference of a hairsbreadth will become the loss of a thousand miles. Man seeks fame and fortune throughout his life and though the way may be present in both, neither fame nor fortune are in themselves the way. The way will never be visible to those who wallow in fame and fortune.

The three mortal worlds of the red dust resemble a furnace in which one's guts boil and the internal organs burn. When, in the grip of the stupidity and ignorance of the external world we suddenly look back, we can see that "he stands in the fading light of the lamp". Like ice in the flames of desire it maintains its pure luster amidst the clamor of the world. This is the true presence of the way of tranquility and clarity.

The Mahayana Buddhist classic, the *Vimalakirti Sutra* says: "That a lotus should blossom in a fire may be said to be rare, to practice Zen amidst desire is also as rare." To turn affliction to bodhi, to transform a sea of fire to a land of coolness and amidst the fires of desire in the mundane world of red dust to cultivate a golden lotus flower that never withers, that is a precious state of mind difficult to attain.

**Huileng**, 854–932, successor to the teachings of Master Yicun of Xuefeng. Lived at the Changqing Monastery in Fuzhou (Fujian province) and was commonly known as Huileng of Changqing.

# 40
## Smashing the Cash Pot
### *Qiji*

*Just stuffing your belly with cash,*
*How can you know its harm?*
*In the end the cash pot must smash,*
*To be taken by others.*

The cash pot is an ancient Chinese pottery receptacle for storing money. There is a hole for putting money in but none for taking it out. When it is full, the pot is smashed and the money retrieved. This short poem is a simple superficial warning of the harm of unlimited greed. Buddhism divides the desires of men into five: wealth, sex, fame, eating and sleeping. The desire for wealth is the most susceptible to harm. The suffering in life is due to insatiable greed. The Tang dynasty essayist Liu Zongyuan, wrote in his satirical essay *The Story of the Fu Beetle* that the beetle desired above all two things: to carry a heavy load and to climb high. It liked carrying things on its back whether or not they were of any use. Even if the load was taken from its back it continued to load itself with useless objects until finally it crushed itself or fell to its death. There is a venerable monk who says that people today are not starved to death, they are stuffed to death. This is a point worth remembering. What is it that stuffs us to death? It is unlimited desire and appetite! When, like the cash pot you are stuffed full of money, that is when calamity strikes. Everybody understands reason, but few manage to put it into practice. In secular society people die for wealth and birds die for food, the car in front in a multiple collision eventually affects the car at the back and everybody stampedes to their death for wealth and profit.

Superficial it may be, but this is a poem that everybody can understand, though from the past right up to the present those who truly understand and can look back have been few indeed.

**Qiji**, c.860–c.937, well-known monk-poet of the Five Dynasties. Lost both parents when young and became a herd-boy for a monastery, later leaving home and taking the tonsure as a monk. Traveled widely and made friends with poets and well-known scholars, reciting poetry, playing the *qin* and drinking.

# 41

## A *Gatha* of Farewell to Life and an Admonition to Disciples
### Zhihui

*My parents built a hut*
*Where I've lived these eighty years.*
*It's dilapidated now*
*And I thought to move.*
*In two minds, between love and hate,*
*I'll wait till it tumbles down*
*And there'll be no barrier*
*Between the two.*

Using the hut as a metaphor for the corporeal body, the poem expresses the Zen monk's mood of vast detachment.

The physical body is the hut that our parents built for us. After living there for 80 years much of it is dilapidated. The 84 year old Zen master feels that his body is less and less fit.

He had intended to move house some time ago and if he did not move on time he would have been torn between love of the new and hatred of the old, which would have been contrary to the Zen belief in non-differentiation.

The house was in a bad state, so nature should take its

course, the house should collapse and physical life come to an end. "Self" moves up naturally to a new home with no barrier between the two.

Buddhism regards the conclusion of mortal life as a "life of the future", the change to a new residence. The kind of house in which you live in the next stage of your life, whether as a Bodhisattva or in the belly of a donkey, depends upon the success of your practice of cultivation.

**Zhihui**, 873–956, a Zen master of the Caodong School of the Five Dynasties. Lived and preached in the Zhongnan hills in Shaanxi.

# 42

# Admiring Flowers Clad in a Woolen Robe
*Wenyi*

> *Clad in a monk's woolen robe,*
> *I admire the flowering blossom.*
> *Today my hair is white,*
> *Last year the flowers were red.*
> *Beauty comes on the morning dew*
> *But fades with the evening breeze.*
> *Why wait for the fallen blossom*
> *To begin to know the void?*

When Li Jing (916–961), the second emperor of the Southern Tang dynasty, welcomed Wenyi to the capital Nanjing, he made him a tutor and frequently consulted him about Buddhism. One day, when they were admiring a tree peony together, the emperor asked him to compose a *gatha* and Wenyi offered him this poem. When he read the poem the emperor achieved enlightenment.

Self, dressed as a monk, faces the tracery of flowers and sees, with the mind of the new-born, all the phenomena of the world, and all that he perceives and feels is clear, deep, and detached, an impression that is utterly different from that of the ordinary person in the secular world. The differing perceptions of the void as seen from the world of form are described below.

In his prime the flower viewer had hair at the temples like dark silk. It is now as white as snow. This year's flowers are as red as last year's, last year's flowers have already withered away, and this year's soon will. Everything is in an ever-changing state of impermanence.

The peony is the king of flowers, luxuriantly fragrant, but its life is as ephemeral as the early morning dew, its fragrance dying away on the evening breeze.

However luxuriant the peony it must wither sooner or later. Why should one wait until it has fallen and become dust and mud before realizing that the essence of glory is just a fistful of sand? To perceive the empty void, the non-existence of things through viewing flowers as they wither signifies the ability to retain a sense of the ordinary that is unmoved and immovable. This is a true freedom from care that has some use.

The *Diamond Sutra* says: "Everything that arises from circumstance resembles floating bubbles of delusion in a dream, like dew and like lightning; the world should be viewed as such." There is no exception to this rule. It covers everything that arises from cause, from animals, plants and sentient beings to rulers and leaders and riches and glory. "The romance of the performance in an open pavilion will always be swept away by the rain and wind!" The Zen master differs from those ordinary people who derive sensory pleasure from the emotional world of physical stimuli and from the gaudiness of the world of emotions. He is able to comprehend and brilliantly elucidate the principle of the essential emptiness of impermanence.

If, as we live amidst the noise and bustle of the world, we can comprehend the nature of the essential emptiness of the sand-like quality of glory, we can experience a mutual imprinting of minds with Zen Master Wenyi.

**Wenyi**, 885–958, late Tang-Five Dynasties, posthumous title Fayan Great Master, founder of the Fayan school.

# 43

## A *Gatha* upon the Styles of Schools
### *Deshao*

*Through mystery to its mountain peak,*
*I'm no longer of this world.*
*There's nothing that lies beyond the mind,*
*Its eyes filled*
*With the blue of hills.*

On the day that you enter a higher state and reach the
mountain peak that leads to truth, when you see the way
and become enlightened, what you experience is totally
beyond the imagination of those who inhabit the mundane
world of red dust at the foot of the hill.

After you have achieved enlightenment and seen the
way, all becomes the self-mind and the self-mind becomes
all. The blue hills that fill the eyes, even the infinity of
natural phenomena are manifestations of the self-nature.
Everything is the product of the self-nature and vice-versa.
Body and mind meld with the hills, rivers and earth as one
entity, a single mind and nothing else.

Composed in a single breath, the magnificent mood
of this poem expresses the realization of "the self-mind is
all and all is the self-mind" and is filled with unbounded
spiritual self sufficiency. Such a *gatha* could not have been

written without a profound personal experience. Deshao's teacher, Zen Master Wenyi, had a very high opinion of it and said: "On the basis of this poem, we can re-vitalize my school's style of teaching."

**Deshao**, 891–972, head disciple under Zen Master Wenyi who made a considerable contribution to the propagation of the teachings of the Fayan school.

# Song Dynasty
## (960–1279)

# 44

## On Tianzhu Mountain
*Zanning*

*In the spacious temple,*
*The back door's not barred at night.*
*Half a gatha composed beside the stream,*
*A remaining sutra read beneath the moon.*
*Though I pursued the mundane dust,*
*I came awake at last.*
*Those who do not know this truth,*
*Must labor in lifelong toil.*

The space and tranquility of the monk's quarters is not disturbed by the mundane world. Walking by the stream whilst composing the half of a *gatha* and reading the remainder of a Buddhist sutra by moonlight portrays the untrammeled detachment and buoyancy of mood of the Zen monk's life. Every living being has lost its original nature amidst the six dusts of form, sound, fragrance, taste, touch and imagination. Consequently they must seek a clarity of awakening from the muddled dreams of dust through self-cultivation. If you do not understand that the ultimate significance of life lies in the goal of awaking to enlightenment, then toiling away in the red dust will always be a waste of effort and will never get anywhere.

The first four lines of the poem describe the scene and events in the hill temple, tranquil and buoyant; the remaining lines point out the goal, outstanding and profound.

**Zanning**, 919–1001, a senior monk of the early Song dynasty. Compiled the *Biographies of Song Senior Monks*, a major contribution to the history of Buddhism in China.

# 45

# The Doctrine from the West
## *Lingcheng*

*A monk asked about the doctrine from the West,*
*I said I'd lived in the mountains I knew not how long.*
*Straw sandals hanging by a thread,*
*And patched hempen robe over my shoulders.*
*From the eastern temple I see the western temple snow,*
*From the spring above flows the stream below.*
*In depth of night the clouds disperse,*
*And the moon shines bright before my window.*

Amongst those who knew the way, not only was there
a lack of concern for the mundane, even an interest in
the arrival in China from Western India of the teachings
of Bodhidharma, the basis of Buddhism and of Zen, was
regarded as superfluous. Consequently when a monk asks
what the doctrine of Zen is, the reply is that he cannot
remember how many years he has lived in the mountains,
he only knows that through meditation and the practice of
Zen in the depths of the hills there had been great changes
and the years had flown by.

Straw sandals were originally secured to the foot by
two "ears" back and front. Now there are only three so the

sandal is not tied on properly ("hanging by a thread") and the wearer can only shuffle. His robe is patched across the shoulders but the Zen monk is content in adversity, happy and beyond material things.

The clouds disperse and bright moonlight shines in front of the window. This window is the canopied window of the Zen master's mountain dwelling and, more to the point, the window to his soul.

The poem describes the plain style of mountain life and its indulgently romantic charm expresses the Zen monk's carefree state of enlightenment.

**Lingcheng**, master of the early Song Yunmen school of Zen. Carefree and unaffected, known as the "carefree sage".

# 46

## The Fly and the Window
### *Shouduan*

*Buzzing against the paper pane,*
*Wanting the light, it never gets through.*
*Suddenly it finds the way it came*
*And knows itself deceived by life.*

The fly sees the light coming in through the window and attempts to get through the window pane but is prevented by the window paper. Innumerable attempts are made everywhere to achieve enlightenment from confusion. The fly's inability to reach the light along the route that it came by is a metaphor for the person armed with the knowledge of the truth, who, however, always departs further from it.

When cause and affinity are ripe, the fly inadvertently comes across the way it came and flies out, thus realizing that in its normal behavior it had been deceived by the eyes of the flesh. Now that its eyes are open it realizes in a moment of enlightenment that there is no life to be won in a pile of old paper.

The poem expresses a profound Zen truth through the ordinary events of life. The fly's search for the light symbolizes the perplexity and eventual enlightenment of the Zen practitioner's search for truth.

**Shouduan**, 1025–1072, skilled in ink painting and calligraphy when young. After leaving home to become a monk promoted Zen teachings at the Haihui Temple at Baiyunshan mountain, Shuzhou (present-day Qianshan in Anhui province). Known as Shouduan of Baiyun.

# 47

# Bidding Farewell to Zhu Daqing
*Fayan*

*If the mind's at ease so is all,*
*In market place or mountain stream.*
*Right and wrong, fame and profit*
*Are suddenly a dream,*
*And when you see them with a wiser eye,*
*They live only for an instant.*

Whether you live in a noisy city or, hermit-like, in the remote mountains, as long as your mind is at ease so, too, will everything else be. With an easy mind, even if you live amidst the clamor of a city, it will seem as if you are living in the tranquil depths of the mountains. With an uneasy mind it will seem like living in the hubbub of a noisy town. With the mind at ease a mountain of red dust becomes no different from the refreshing cool of a bodhimanda, a place of enlightenment. With an uneasy or troubled mind, the bodhimanda is transformed into a mountain of red dust.

The mind filled with anxiety is always engaged, always toiling away and busy without achievement. Seen with the wisdom of the eyes of the true Buddhist law, right and wrong and fame and profit are illusory bubbles in a dream, wisps of smoke before the eyes. To be able to see through right and wrong and fame and profit is to be at ease and free of care; if you cannot, it is as if the vital organs were on fire.

Dislike clamor or thirst for tranquility no longer: the mind and all else are at ease. Break through the barrier of right and wrong and fame and profit, and wake from the dream.

**Fayan**, ?–1104, studied under Zen Master Shouduan at the Baiyun Temple and later succeeded him. Moved to the founder's Dongshan Temple at Qizhou and was known as the Fifth Patriarch of Qizhou. Also known as Master Fifth Patriarch.

## 48

## Roaming the Bell Mountain
*Wang Anshi*

*Gazing at the hills all day I never tire,*
*I think to buy a hill and spend my old age there.*
*When all the flowers have fallen,*
*The hill remains there still,*
*The streams themselves flow on,*
*The hill itself at ease.*

In his old age, Wang Anshi lived as a hermit at Half Hill
Garden outside Nanjing, the burdens of office already
in the past of the secular world. The Wang Anshi of this
period had a particularly intimate feeling for natural
scenery.

The poet gazes at the hill all day and the more he
looks the more he likes it and is moved to buy it, hoping
to spend the remainder of his years there. "The man of
humanity takes joy in the hills" and the hills are tall and
majestic, broad and ample, just the kind of mountain
characteristics that Wang Anshi appreciated in his old age.

It is not enough for the poet to look at the hills.
He wishes to spend his old age there because he is
fascinated and moved by their inner quality. In the hills
the flowers bloom and wither, the water from the springs

flows on without cease and the hill remains unmoved, a metaphor for all living things, some in a state of flux and impermanence, others majestically immoveable. Rich and poor, noble and base, glory and disgrace, profit and loss, all resemble the mountain flowers and streams as they bloom and wither and bloom again and as they flow back and forth, while the hills remain unchanged and unchanging. This hill is our original mind and true nature. When we come to comprehend these two, mind and nature, we can be calm, settled and at ease, undisturbed by the secular world.

The word "hill" occurs four times in the poem, twice in each sentence, giving a sense of reciprocal repetition and powerfully emphasizing the natural calm of Zen joy and leisurely contentment in the unity of the poet and the hill.

**Wang Anshi**, 1021–1086, Northern Song politician, thinker, poet and essayist. Prime minister under emperor Shenzong and introduced reforms. Twice dismissed. Retired as a hermit to Banshan (Half Hill) near Jiangning (present-day Nanjing in Jiangsu province). Became a Buddhist in late life when the style of his poetry underwent a considerable change. He wrote a large number of Zen poems.

# 49

# Thinking of the Past with Brother Ziyou at Mianchi
### Su Shi

*In all, what does life resemble?*
*It seems a goose print in the slush of snow.*
*That chance left footprint will soon be gone,*
*And the goose flies it knows not where.*
*The old monk is dead, his new stupa built*
*And nowhere to see old poems*
*On the temple's crumbling walls.*
*Do you remember the rugged paths,*
*The weariness of the long road*
*And the braying of the donkey?*

On his way to take up a post in Shaanxi province, Su Shi passed through Mianchi (in present Henan province). His younger brother, Su Zhe, saw him off as far as Zhengzhou and then returned to the capital Kaifeng. Out of brotherly concern and because it was difficult to see him further on his way, Su Zhe wrote a poem, *Remembering Mianchi, a Poem for Elder Brother Zizhan* and presented it to him. The present highly regarded poem is its partner, a *qilü*, a Chinese poem of eight lines with seven characters in each. It is the origin of the well known saying: "A goose print in the slush," meaning the ephemeral nature of life or a trace of the past. The poem is suffused with a sense of the impermanence of life and the need to treasure affinity.

We live in this world, drifting hither and thither, but what is it really like? It is like the imprint of a goose's webbed foot in the slush of snow.

By chance an imprint is left in the slush but the goose that made it has long flown, its whereabouts unknown. The imprint is everything that we leave in the world: house, car, reputation, achievement, writings, they are all footprints in the slush, shortly to be consigned to oblivion. What is more, the you that is the flying goose may soon pass away to an altered form of life.

Looking back at the past, it is as fragile and impermanent as the goose's footprint in the slush. The old monk has died, a new stupa has been added to the forest of stupas and the old poems have been obliterated from the walls of the Buddhist temple. Like the old monk, the poems have disappeared without trace.

This poem was written five years after Su Shi took up his post. The poet recalls the circumstances of the journey that year, its length, the weariness of the travelers and the braying of the exhausted donkey. The hardships of those days are now caught by the reminiscences of the poet's brush and filled with a comforting fragrance. All life is a footprint in the slush as is each step in life. Each meeting between brothers is precious. But the desperation of the past has become the fond memory of the present.

**Su Shi**, 1037–1101, style name Zizhan, also known as Su Dongpo. Northern Song literary figure, calligrapher and artist. Gained doctoral degree (*jinshi*) during the reign of emperor Jiayou (1056–1063) and served as Secretary of the Board of Rites. Demoted several times because of his opposition to the reforms of Wang Anshi. Outstandingly talented, perceptive and quick-witted, he left a large number of Zen poems and other fine works.

# 50

## A Poem for Mr Shen's *Qin*

### *Su Shi*

*If the sound of the* qin
*Lies in its strings,*
*Why is it not heard*
*Inside the box?*
*If you say it's in the fingers,*
*Why don't I hear it from yours?*

Only contact between finger and string can produce a
beautiful sound from the *qin* (an instrument that resembles
a kind of plucked dulcimer). No sound can be produced by
strings without fingers or by fingers without strings. This
poem vividly conveys a realization of the original ideas of
Buddhism.

The *Madh Yamagama Sutra* says: "If this exists then that
exists also, if this does not exist then that does not exist
either, if this is destroyed then that also is destroyed."
The whole universe and all that is within is one whole
life and is the result of the combination of causes. The
*Surangama Sutra* says: "For example, though the *qin*, *se* and
*pipa* produce a fine sound, they cannot do so without fine
fingers. You and all sentient beings are thus." The mind
of every sentient being possesses a Buddha-nature, but

without the "fine fingers" of the teachings of the Buddha, the sentient beings wallowing in the five desires will never be able to discover the Buddha-nature that is within them.

In *A Poem for Zen Master Shen upon Hearing the Jialing River*, Wei Yingwu wrote:

"The nature of water is still
And rock has no sound.
How is it that when the two clash,
Rolling thunder
Shocks the empty hills?"

Water and stone are fundamentally still, it is only when altitude and terrain cause the river water to clash with the rock that sound is produced. Were there no combination of cause between water and rock there would be no reason for sound from the water. There is nothing in the world that is not like this.

Each and every phenomenon of the world arises from cause. The beauty of a flower requires the life of the universe to accomplish it. Everything that belongs to each of us today depends upon the accomplishment of affinity. Consequently, we must treasure all who cross our life's horizons with compassion, support them and accomplish together, not undermine or harm them.

# 51

## Staying at the Donglin Temple
### Su Shi

*If the sound of water is its fluent tongue,*
*Then the mountain is its tranquil body.*
*Eighty four thousand gatha in a night,*
*How can I pass them on?*

Throughout the night the murmuring water of the stream
ceaselessly proclaims the subtleties of the Buddhist law and
the green clad mountain presents the pure body of the law
in all its clarity.

In the course of one night, the stream flows like a
jewel announcing the 84,000 teachings of the Buddha; they
contain such a wealth of wisdom—how can a mere three
inch tongue pass on the detail of their mystery to others?
Moreover, "There is a truth in all of this, / A mystery
for which I lack the words." Even if one were to try to
expound only a part, there are no normal words that can
express it.

The *Surangama Sutra* says: "If you can metamorphose
the material then you will become an enlightened Buddha."
If the mind can metamorphose the material then it follows
that the sound of admiration and the sound of slander, the
sound of water and of wind, the sound of birds and insects,

the shrieking of demons and the howling of wolves all fall easily on the ear and are the most wonderful of the names of the Buddha. There is a stone monument beside a bridge at the back of the Guanghua Temple on which is inscribed a *gatha* by the Qing dynasty hermit, Peng Jiqing: "We sit on the bridge, / The water flows beneath. / Fervently thank the water, / For reciting Amitabha for me." To the ears of those who pray to Buddha the tinkling sound of the water sounds like the name of the Amitabha Buddha, an expression of the mood of those who pray.

It is the same to the knowledgeable eye. If the mountain landscape is the pure body, then other forms, too, are also the pure body. No matter whether people are male or female, young or old, of high status or low, attractive or not, rich or poor, noble or base, emperor or beggar, they should all be regarded as reincarnations of the Dharma-body of the Amitabha Buddha. In this way, everything that we see before our eyes is the Buddha body.

# 52

# Gazing at the Tide
## Su Shi

*The mists on Lushan and the Zhe river tide.*
*Before I saw them I felt regret.*
*Now I've seen them my mind's at rest,*
*The mists on Lushan and the Zhe river tide.*

This poem expresses the imagery of feeling in the three stages in Zen enlightenment.

In the first stage of practice which precedes enlightenment, mountains are seen as mountains and water is seen as water and it is only possible to see an object's external form and not the true form that stands behind it. Through practice and on reaching the second stage, mountains are seen as not mountains and water is seen as not water. Whatever the eye beholds or the mind feels is a false image distorted by one's own consciousness. There is still no perception of the true image. Before actually reaching the true image, life is full of regret.

The practitioner of Zen continues his arduous practice, finally achieves sudden enlightenment and sees that mountains are only mountains and that water is only water. It is only at this point that he really arrives at the essence of things, and comes into the possession of a pure mind and deep understanding and can take joy in the beauty of everything that the world contains.

Nothing at all has changed in itself, there has been no change in the circumstances of life. It is just that the feelings before and after enlightenment are completely different and it is the nature of the beholder that has changed. The act of enlightenment has caused a return to the state that existed before one lost one's way.

# 53

## The Hot Spring

### *Kezun*

*In the Zen temple,*
*Who carved the dragon head spout*
*From whose mouth*
*The hot spring waters gush?*
*Once all beings are cleansed of dust,*
*Then clear and cool again,*
*I'll mingle with the stream once more.*

The poet inscribed this poem on the wall of a temple at the foot of the Lushan mountain during a visit.

The Buddhist temple had a hot spring where one of the monks had chiseled out the shape of a dragon's head and placed it at the spot where the hot spring discharged its water, so that the spring water emerged through the dragon's mouth.

The Zen master compares himself to the hot spring water and says that since he is a Buddhist disciple, he has a duty towards ordinary sentient beings and a willingness to cleanse their body and mind of dust and filth. Moreover, after all beings are clean of dust, "I" will happily retire from success and unassumingly turn to clear cool water to become one with the ordinary stream water.

"I swear not to become a Buddha until hell is empty"—
the compassionate Buddhist Mahayana spirit of self-
sacrificing altruism of the poem wins our admiration. But
we can also appreciate the author's indication that after his
task is complete he is no different from anybody else.

**Kezun**, Song dynasty monk. Skilled poet, who often
exchanged poems with Su Shi and others.

# 54

# An Answer to Kezun

*Liaoyuan*

*All those thousands who seek Zen*
*Often drowse*
*And in their dreams chase profit*
*Like a wisp of smoke.*
*Rouse yourself to gain Zen calm*
*It's as deep as the sleep*
*Of a silkworm.*

Buddhist monks in their thousands sleep during the day. Sleeping and dreaming are closely connected. One should not sleep during the day, particularly if one dreams of fame and profit. The practitioner should "shake himself free of affliction, rid himself of greed and fame, in shaking himself like a blanket, he can rid himself of dust and filth". Concentrate the mind on a single point in meditation to discard distraction.

The Zen master says that he has already entered old age where Zen calm resembles the sleep of a silkworm in its length. The pupating silkworm neither eats nor moves in a sleep-like state known as silkworm hibernation. This second stage sleep of the silkworm is a metaphor for the lengthy time of the state of settled Zen calm, implying the need to discard the sense of fame and profit and eliminate distractions in order to achieve the state of true Zen calm.

**Liaoyuan**, 1022–1086, honorific Foyin. Abbot of the Jinshan Monastery at Zhenjiang. Poet and calligrapher. Associate of Su Dongpo (Su Shi), Huang Shangu and others. Emperor Shenzong granted him the title of "Imprint of the Buddha".

## 55

## An Extempore Verse
*Daoqian*

*Send to ask that pretty girl in the eastern hills,*
*To tease the dreams of King Xiang of Chu.*
*Like a mud-laden willow frond,*
*My Zen mind does not dance*
*To the spring wind's jaunty tune.*

Daoqian called on Su Shi when he was an official in
Xuzhou. At a banquet Su Shi persuaded a singing girl to ask
Daoqian for a poem. To the astonishment of those present
Daoqian extemporized this poem on the spot, gaining
much fame thereby. The poem expresses the solid practice
skills of the Zen mind.

The first two lines of the poem ask this pretty and
attractive girl to tease Hermit Su (Su Shi) who resembles
the romantically inclined King Xiang of Chu. The
remaining lines are an expression of will: my Zen mind is
like a mud-laden frond of willow that will not float in the
air however much the spring wind blows. Once the willow
fronds are covered in mud the spring wind does not blow
again. Daoqian uses this as a metaphor for the gentleness
of his own nature, one not susceptible to being teased
by beauty. The phrase "mud-laden fronds of willow" was

subsequently used to describe the uninterested, detached and somewhat weary fashion in which the Zen mind regarded the red dust.

In life, however, the ability to pass even more severe tests is the mark of a master at the summit.

According to the *Collection of the Hard Gourd* by the Qing dynasty writer Chu Renhuo, Su Dongpo (Su Shi) used to take singing girls to the Jinshan monastery and drink with Foyin, the abbot, making him completely drunk. Finally he induced a pretty girl to go to bed with the abbot, while he slept elsewhere. When Foyin woke, he declined the blandishments of the girl with a poem: "Drunk at night and so to bed, / Unaware, a lute beside my pillow. / Tell that Hanlin Scholar Su, / I didn't pluck a single string!" Thus demonstrating the strength of will of the Zen mind.

**Daoqian**, 1043–1102, style name Canliao. Left home in his youth and became a monk at the Qiantang Temple. A friend and boon companion of Su Shi and known for his poetry. When Su Shi was demoted and exiled to south China, Daoqian was also implicated and ordered to return to secular life. He later returned to monk-hood.

# 56
## Tapping
### *Rubi*

*Tock, tock, tock.*
*An insect's inside,*
*And there's pecking outside.*
*All those people drowsing away,*
*Don't know there's an awl on top.*
*Fail to wake and you'll hear the monk above,*
*Tock, tock, tocking.*

Once, when he was preaching, Zen Master Rubi heard
the sound of a bird tapping on a tree outside the temple
and used the sound to present a *gatha* to the assembled
monks. The language of the *gatha* uses the sound of the
woodpecker (tock, tock, tock) to stimulate people's
awareness. The preacher explains that people only have
to lack awareness for a single day and he will then have to
endlessly preach the Buddhist law.

The insect represents affliction and ignorance and the
woodpecker's tapping to get at it, represents the shattering
of the students' affliction and ignorance through the use
of harsh methods. Zen is accustomed to using actions such
as "the awl on top" as a metaphor for the strong measures
taken to dispel the confusion of students and stimulate

their sense of awareness.

Whilst there have always been many practitioners of Zen, few have achieved enlightenment. The direct, speedy attainment of enlightenment always requires the practitioner to endure "the awl on top". While you are being tapped away at, the insect of greed, anger and ignorance is being pecked out and consumed. An enlightened life can only really be revived when age-old ignorance has been thoroughly stripped out and evil knowledge and views crushed.

**Rubi**, 1065–1129, became a monk after several unsuccessful attempts at the imperial exams. An erudite literary figure particularly skilled in poetry. A member of the Jiangxi school of poetry (which emphasized the poet's right to originality). Regarded by Lu You as first among monk-poets.

# 57
## No Gain
*Kongyan You*

*It's always piles of gold*
*In our dreams.*
*A greed for wealth and honor*
*Difficult to curb.*
*When the pillow falls*
*And you suddenly wake,*
*The cold wind blows about you,*
*With no place for dreams.*

In their dreams, most people pursue wealth and honor.
A Tang dynasty scholar called Lu was asleep in an inn
on a journey and dreamed that he had gone up in the
world, become an official and had made his fortune;
another scholar asleep under a locust tree dreamed he
had been become the son-in-law of the ruler of the state
of South Kui and governor of the province of Nanke,
acquiring honor and children and grandchildren. Ordinary
people who dream of these situations are usually beside
themselves with joy.

There is always a waking from dreams, the pillow falls
and you wake at once. The Tang scholar dreaming at the

inn found that when he woke his millet had not yet boiled, though in his short dream he had experienced a lifetime of wealth and honor—this is the millet dream. The scholar dreaming under the locust tree found himself demoted and dishonored just as he was at the height of his glory and cried out in distress, waking to find the state of South Kui was an ant's nest beneath the tree—this is the Nanke dream. The scenery of the dream is limitless, but the waking scene is desolate, the room utterly empty with just the cold wind on all sides brushing your tears.

As we wallow in the red dust, wealth and honor are always a dream. Life itself is like a dream and one should not network for personal gain. In everyday life, the occasions on which one attends one's own funeral through the greedy and improper acquisition of money are too numerous to mention. This is why one remains immersed in a dream of ignorance unable to wake. Enlightenment can only occur on waking.

**Kongyan You**, Song dynasty monk of whose life nothing is known.

# 58
## A Youthful Romance
### *Keqin*

*Within the embroidered curtain*
*The gilded burner's incense drifts.*
*Drunk from the midst of music*
*By others supported home.*
*This romance of youth*
*Only one beauty knows.*

Before he wrote this poem Keqin had heard his teacher, Zen Master Fayan, preach about Zen on a text of two lines from a poem describing the scene in the bridal chamber on a wedding night: "Calling her handmaid without cause, / Only wishing her husband to know her voice."

In ancient China, there was no direct contact between men and women and a woman could not take the initiative in expressing delight to a man, nor could she loudly call to her husband. Consequently the new bride waiting for her husband in the bridal chamber frequently called to her maid to serve tea in order to attract her husband's attention and to let him know that she was there and waiting for him. The thoughtfulness of all Buddhas resembles the actions of the bride, and all sentient beings who receive the call resemble the groom. The teachings of the Buddhas and the sayings and *koan* of the ancient masters resonate in the summons to the maid. Master Fayan used this erotic verse to hint to those with the understanding that the path to the realization of the way lay through enlightenment.

As he heard these two lines, Keqin grasped their meaning, wrote this erotic poem and presented it to his master. The shyness of the young woman in articulating the intoxication of passion is a metaphor for the Zen that cannot be put into words. It symbolizes the particular method of transmission, through the impression of mind upon mind, that exists between teacher and disciple.

The smoke of incense drifts up from the gilded burner and is lost within the embroidered curtain, and oneself, helplessly drunk, is supported home from the banquet. Thinking back on the romantic episode he has just experienced, the young man's heart is filled with joy. He knows that only "the beauty" with whom he shared the romantic experience is fully aware of its private and mutual joy. In the metaphor for the state of Zen enlightenment, only two people know its implications, oneself and one's teacher.

The state of Zen enlightenment can be compared to the passion of a young man in love, as in drinking water only oneself knows. The young man's feelings can only be sensed by the girl who loves him. The call of the Buddha to all sentient beings and the call of the teacher to his disciple can only be heard by those with the Buddha-nature in their hearts.

Fayan read this erotic poem with its incense-laden overtones and happily gave it his approval.

**Keqin**, 1063–1135, left home to become a monk when young. Studied with Fifth Patriarch Fayan and lived at the Zhaojue Temple in Chengdu. In April 1127, after the Jurchen army attacked and took the capital Dongjing (present-day Kaifeng in Henan province) leading to the fall of the Northern Song dynasty, the southern Song emperor, Gaozong, summoned him to discuss military affairs and conferred on him the title of Master of Perfect Enlightenment. His *Record of the Blue Cliff* is regarded as the "first book of Zen".

# 59

## A Gift in Parting
### *Zonggao*

*Knock out the bottom of the barrel*
*To see the world's extent.*
*Sever the roots of life*
*And see the clear blue pool.*
*Take snow from the blazing furnace,*
*To sprinkle amongst men*
*As a lamp to shine at night.*

Zen uses the metaphor of the "black lacquer barrel" to
represent the speck of lacquer black in the brains of the
unenlightened and the removal of the bottom of the barrel
to represent the state of enlightenment. When the bottom
of the barrel is knocked out, you can see the vastness of the
world. Severing the roots of life refers to the solution of
the problem of opposites like life and death and symbolizes
enlightenment. When the veritable truth appears one
can cultivate oneself to the state of clarity of a blue pool,
thereby escaping all the restrictions that bind to give birth
to a feeling of incomparable vastness and light.

The blazing furnace that burns so fiercely is the world
of affliction and suffering and the snow with its luster of
purity is a symbol of the Buddha-nature. The mission of

the Zen practitioner is to point out the Buddha-nature that lies hidden in the world of suffering and to help those who seek freedom to illuminate their own path.

The poem is filled with energy and a burning emotion. It is a Zen poem that contains the true ability of the Buddha and reveals the transcendental joy of the poet's own enlightenment and his ardor, once enlightened, for the deliverance of all sentient beings from suffering and difficulty.

Zonggao acted upon the aspirations that he expressed in the poem. In the history of Zen he stands as a Zen master with a substantial achievement in teaching. The records of the Zen school indicate that more than 90 of those that he had trained and taught subsequently achieved enlightenment. This is an unprecedented and unsurpassed record.

**Zonggao**, 1089–1163, honorific Miaoxi. Succeeded to the mantle of Master Keqin. Loyal and courageous in conduct with a reputation for eloquence. The Song emperor Xiaozong awarded him the title "Dahui" (Great Wisdom) and made him abbot of the Jingshan Temple in Zhejiang province.

## 60

## For the Practitioner

*Tanhua*

*Better to nurse the mind*
*Than the body.*
*The body is content*
*With a nourished mind.*
*When body and mind*
*Are nourished both,*
*Then immortal already,*
*What need of further honor?*

In modern society, the pace of life is becoming faster
and faster, the pressures are heavier and heavier, there
are more and more attractions and greater pollution and
physical and mental illness is more widespread. Despite
developments in modern medicine there are still many
conditions for which there is no cure because mental
illness requires medicine of the mind. Consequently, just
nourishing the physical body will never be sufficient. Only
by nourishing the mind will the body avoid illness. Chinese
medicine says: "Anger damages the liver, an excess of joy
damages the heart, introspection damages the spleen, grief
damages the lungs and fear damages the kidneys." Thus

it can be seen that physical illness derives from mental illness.

Although physical illness derives in the main from mental illness, nevertheless, the absence of a healthy body leaves the spirit with nothing to depend upon. Consequently care of the body is important. The ideal is a body and mind that are both cultivated to the greatest possible extent. At this point you are already almost a happy immortal in heaven with no further need to seek low-level satisfaction in honor upon earth.

**Tanhua**, 1103–1163, Song dynasty monk of the Linji (Rinzai) school, honorific Ying'an. Known with Dahui Zonggao as the two outstanding Buddhist personalities of the Linji school.

# 61

# Three Zen Masters Visit the Guoqing Temple
*Zhiyu*

> *Who knows*
> *Three hermits in their solitude,*
> *Sought old friends*
> *To bid farewell at Eagle Peak.*
> *In parting at the temple gate,*
> *Each bamboo leaf*
> *Rustled its own cool breeze.*

The cultivated bamboo symbolizes the character of the host. At the conclusion of tea drinking and while the host is seeing off his guests at the gate, the gleaming green leaves of the bamboo appear to sense his intentions and dance gently in the breeze with a rustling sound as if also bidding the departing guests a fond farewell, engaging us with the depth of feeling between friends.

The poem also brings an understanding of the solemn idea of "once in a lifetime".

"Once in a lifetime" was originally a phrase from the Warring States period of Japanese history, meaning that one should bring to bear the whole of one's being upon the act of drinking the bowl of tea in front of you, hence "once in a lifetime". Before samurai went into battle, the general would invite a tea master to perform the tea ceremony for them. They did not know whether they would return from the battlefield alive and temporarily set aside the cruelty of battle and concentrated their whole spirit upon the actual and irretrievable moment before them. This was also the only way to banish fear and unease.

"Once in a lifetime" reminds us to treasure the opportunities present in each moment and, because it may be the only encounter of a lifetime, to put the whole of one's heart into it. If, through indifference, the meeting is neglected, it may lead to a lifetime of regret. Life is a coming together and dispersal and a dispersal and coming together, no two meetings are identical. Not only is it difficult to meet up with close friends, it is even more difficult to meet with oneself, so one should treasure it all the more.

**Zhiyu**, 1184–1269, Buddhist honorific Xutang, well known monk of the Southern Song dynasty. Lived and preached successively at the well-known temples of Yuwang, Jingci and Jingshan where he had many adherents, almost filling the halls beyond capacity. The king of Goryeo (Korea) invited him for a stay that lasted eight years.

# 62

## A Poem upon Enlightenment
*Anonymous Nun*

*Treading in straw sandals*
*Amid the cloud set peaks,*
*Searching all day for the spring*
*I could not find.*
*Exhausted I return,*
*And smiling caress a flower,*
*To breathe the plum blossom's scent,*
*And find spring ten parts full*
*At the tip of a stem.*

Clad in straw sandals and searching strenuously amongst the misty peaks, no trace of spring is to be found. This is a metaphor for the countless practitioners of Zen who, unafraid of hardship, fruitlessly search the hills and dales. Where is the way and where is spring?

Returning unsuccessful and exhausted, the poet sees a winter plum in the courtyard. She touches and smells it, the scent fills the air and she discovers with delight that all along spring has been blossoming on a stem of winter plum, so spring had been on her doorstep!—Everybody possesses an abundance of the Buddha-nature. It need not be sought outside but how many people are capable of comprehending this?

As we seek truth, seek the way, seek our own nature and happiness, our eyes are always fixed outwards and our footsteps wander away, unaware that we should search within ourselves. We seek what we cannot have and ignore what we have, this is back to front and upside down. In reality, the truth, the way, our own nature and happiness, all that we seek so hard, the most treasured things on earth, are not to be found in heaven but with us. What we search so hard for is the priceless jewel that we already possess but do not value.

"The Buddha is within us all, no need to seek afar, it is in our heart. Each of us has a Buddha-nature, and enlightenment proceeds from within."

The way is not further than man and must be found within our own heart. We must return to the present and start with the heart.

**Anonymous Nun**, Southern Song, no details.

# 63

# In Praise of the Way Within the Ordinary Mind
### *Huikai*

*Spring flowers and autumn moon,*
*Summer breeze and winter snow.*
*An unencumbered mind*
*Is man's best season.*

"Spring flowers and autumn moon, / Summer breeze and winter snow." There are four seasons to the year, each with its own scenic beauty. The scenery warms the heart and raises the spirits. Not only does each season have its own beauty but even if the setting remains the same the seasons are different. In his *Notes from the Pavilion of a Drunken Man* the Song dynasty historian Ouyang Xiu said: "The wild flowers of spring compete in blossom and the secluded scent overcomes us; in summer the trees spread in leaf and thickly shade the ground; in autumn the wind is cold, the frost is crisp and the heavens clear and bright; in winter the water drops and the rocks appear, as if clothed in silver." The Northern Song artist, Guo Xi, in *The Forest Spring*, described the characteristics of the four seasons as: "The hills in spring seem as light as a smile (the pale but bright color of the hills), in summer they are a verdant green and appear like a drop of water, in the autumn bright and clear as an ornament, and in winter dismal and asleep." The Ming artist and calligrapher, Shen Hao, in *Hua Zhu*, his treatise on painting said: "The hills in spring are a celebration, in summer a competition, in autumn an illness and in winter a calm (the Zen calm of an old monk)."

An encumbrance is something that inhibits the normal mind or wastes wisdom. If the mirror of the soul is obscured by dust and filth, everything that is reflected in it loses its original shape. In this world those whose minds are unencumbered are truly difficult to find. The Song poet, Lu You, said in *Dispelling Melancholy*: "If you can wash away worldly notions, upon what tower will the moon not shine?" In truth, what is lacking in the ordinary person is not beautiful scenery but the eyes, attitude and frame of mind that can distinguish it. If we can rid our minds of the things that encumber them, then we shall be able to live in a season where we can enjoy the world in all places at all times, and experience a life where every day is a good day.

**Huikai**, 1183–1260, style name Wumen. Achieved enlightenment from the Zen Master of Zhaozhou through the use of the "*wu*" koan. In 1229 he compiled the *Gateless Gate* for the emperor's birthday, one of the three great classics of Zen, on a level with the *Record of the Blue Cliff* and the *Images of Herding Ten Oxen*.

# Modern and Contemporary

## (1840–present)

## 64

## A True Story

*Su Manshu*

*A fairy with a graceful gait*
*And skin of snow,*
*Came close and asked*
*For a poem upon her leaf of red.*
*With a heartless tear I replied,*
*Why did we not meet*
*Before my monkish head was shaved?*

The greatest regret of life is to meet the right person at the wrong time. Even if feelings are deep, you may be destined to meet but fated to part because you are promised to Buddha and no longer belong to the world of passion. Consequently, the tender advances of female beauties must be turned away with a heartless tear, regretting that you had not met before your head was shaved and you became a monk. Here the "heartless" tears contain both melancholy and helplessness.

Su Manshu's good looks and poetic air attracted the adoration of women. However, since he was a monk he distanced himself from the seas of emotion, though deep down, his amorous inclinations were never eradicated or the affinities of love abandoned. Throughout his life, this was a great obstacle to enlightenment causing him frequent bouts of misery from which he found it difficult to escape. Although in his poetry, Su Manshu claimed "Not to plant the roots of love in the field of passion", the reverse was true and his greatest problem was "Not snapping off the roots of love in the field of passion". Unless the roots of love are snapped off, it is difficult to achieve a state of true enlightenment. He was a successful monk in terms of feeling but a failure in terms of practice. Not in his whole life did he ever have the skill to traverse the pass of passion.

**Su Manshu**, 1884–1918, well-known monk-poet of the late-Qing/early-Republic. Studied in Japan for a while. His life was dismal and his mental state painful. However, the artistry of his poetry reached the realms of Buddha.

## 65
## Deathbed *Gatha*
### *Hongyi*

*You asked me whither?*
*My mind so vast with awakening*
*That words are forgotten.*
*Flowering twigs blossom with the sense of spring*
*And the heavens so clear that the rounded moon*
*grows larger.*

This was sent by Master Hongyi to his close friend, the publisher and translator Xia Mianzun. According to Lin Ziqing's *Chronology of Master Hongyi*, Master Hongyi wrote a testamentary letter to Xia Mianzun in which he said: "Hermit Xia Mianzun, I will pass on on the 4th of September, I append two *gatha* as a gift." Sang Rou in his *The Spirituality of Li Shutong*, said: "On a certain morning in the middle of September 1942 (lunar calendar) Xia Mianzun received a registered letter at his office at the translation bureau of the Kaiming Bookshop. It was from Hongyi... The letter very matter-of-factly referred to 'passing on' and bore the sense of a farewell message: 'I've gone, the poems are a memento' with the barely conceivable implication of prior knowledge of the date of death. Xia Mianzun immediately telegraphed the Kaiyuan monastery to enquire and learned that Hongyi had indeed passed away on the 4th of September." This accurate prior knowledge of the date of death casts a mystical light over the *gatha* and has drawn endless praise for it.

Born from whence, why are we here and whither death, are three great questions of concern to all religions. This *gatha* answers the question of whither death and expresses it well. The poem says, you ask me where I am going now, my mind has opened up in a flash of enlightenment. I had originally intended to tell you, but in the state of Zen, rather as in drinking water you instinctively sense hot and cold, one forgets in a moment from where to start speaking. This is a mental state of leisure, ease and calm.

Zen may not speak it but a friend must say it in farewell. Not just in any ordinary fashion but presented in a mood of beauty. See, the flower twigs blossom, there is a sense of spring; the heavens seem washed clean and the shining moon is at its fullest! This perfect place of limitless tranquility and utter peace is the home to which I must return! How pure the scene, how untroubled, how perfect, how aesthetic!

The concept presented by the *gatha* is a sense or feeling frequently experienced by Zen monks in their travels: "You wish to know your place of final return? North East South and West see the willows clothed in silken green." (Zen Master Shuiyue)

"The bubble proceeds from water and returns thither, that I enter this world and I leave it is a matter of normality." (Zen Master Zhiduan)

"How precious the water that flows by the grass-covered river bank, you return to the ocean vastness and I to the mountains." (Zen Master Qinghuo)

"Now packed and prepared for return to where, for ever, the rivers flow and the heavens are blue." (Zen Master Daoji)

The meaning of all these *gatha* is that nothing is permanent, there is life and extinction and coming and going. This is a matter of predestined affinity. Thus we must follow the changes of affinity and not cling to our mortal flesh. Death is a kind of return. When we abandon the minor me and our fleshly body we can indissolubly meld the individual life with that of the cosmos so that it becomes one.

These *gatha* are written with a fluent and accomplished skill and style. In comparison, that of Master Hongyi is denser, more concise, restrained and thought provoking. The more you think on it the more you come to love it.

The *Heart Sutra* says: "When the heart is without anxiety or obstruction then there is no fear, when confusion and illusion are distant, that is true *Nirvana*." When Master Hongyi wrote this *gatha* he had already reached "true *Nirvana*", the state of "neither being nor extinction, neither filth nor purity, neither increase nor diminution".

**Hongyi**, 1880–1942, ordinary surname Li, given name Shutong. Studied in Japan, returned home and took up a position as a teacher of western music and art. He excelled as a composer, artist, calligrapher, seal carver and playwright. Later at the height of his powers became a monk and propagated the teachings of the Lü School of Buddhism that advocated spiritual discipline and restraint. He became the great master of modern Buddhist studies.

# 66

## A *Gatha* upon Seeing the Way
### *Xuyun*

*A tea bowl falls and smashes*
*Like a thunderclap.*
*The void too shatters*
*And wanton desires expire.*

The monk Xuyun wrote this poem in 1895, at the age of 55 in a sudden moment of inspiration at the conclusion of a seven day retreat devoted to Zen calm at the Gaomin Temple near Yangzhou. At that point, all deluded thought was quiescent and day and night had become one. One evening as he was burning incense he opened his eyes and saw a radiance as bright as day and he comprehended everything, both internally and externally. He could see as far as the boats sailing on the Yangtze River and the trees on the banks, all with absolute clarity. On the evening of the third day, those keeping the vigil were boiling water and carelessly spilled some on his hand, so that he dropped the tea bowl with a crash, shattering his doubts and bringing enlightenment. He thereupon wrote this poem.

The ancients could achieve sudden enlightenment at the sound of a cock crowing or a dog barking, at the sound of rubble striking bamboo, or of a river, or of drops of rain, or at the sight of a peach tree, or of cassia flowers. The monk Xuyun had already accumulated much skill over the years and was able to use the moment of opportunity presented by the splash of boiling water and the smashing of the bowl on the ground to achieve sudden enlightenment.

Zen often uses the phrase "The void shatters, the land disappears" to describe the feeling of enlightenment. It means that after one has found one's nature, the myriad worlds dissolve, delusions disappear and there is nothing beyond the mind, everything else is fantasy.

The enlightenment of Master Xuyun was an extremely important event in the history of Chinese Zen. The enlightened Xuyun became a generation of Zen masters. Most Zen monasteries today in China continue in the traditions of his teaching.

When, over the days, months and years, you have accumulated and deepened your skills, any event can be the stimulus for sudden enlightenment. Master Xuyun joins the great worthies and patriarchs of Zen as a shining example.

**Xuyun**, 1840–1959, the guiding star of modern Zen. Left home to become a monk at the age of 19. He laboriously followed the way and practices of Zen for a whole century, set up 15 bodhimanda (places of enlightenment) and rebuilt six foundation temples. His disciples and adherents were numbered in their millions. His 120 years of life, added to legendary experience, combined to give him immense prestige in Buddhist circles.

# Translator's Postscript

There are difficulties to the translation of poetry in any language. These difficulties are multiplied many times when the language is Chinese and when the cultural and philosophical gap is as wide as it is between Chinese and English. The problems are exacerbated when the subject matter is as esoteric as Zen Buddhism.

The translator has to convey the sense of a poem as a whole without damaging the original imagery, or reducing the poem to a mere paraphrase that expresses the meaning without the beauty or profundity of the original. It is a task in which success is never complete and in which the result can never fully represent the richness and color of the original. What the translator sets before the English reader is often only a pale shadow of what the Chinese reader sees and understands.

The three principles of Chinese translation are *xin* (信) integrity or faith to the original, *da* (达) expression or mastery of the content, and *ya* (雅) elegance but also correctness. *Xin* is clearly the most important of these, though it is possible to produce translations which appears technically faithful to the original but which lack integrity because they have not caught its spirit. They observe the principles of *da* and *ya* but lack *xin*.

Nevertheless, the act of translating poetry is often a matter of compromise between competing principles where the letter of accurate translation can sometimes offend the spirit of the whole. The translator of genius transcends this so that the result has poetic integrity and works in English and yet is faithful to the original and, above all, moves the reader of English just as the original moved the Chinese reader. In the end, however, more practical guidance for the translator might be found in the remarks of the eminent 20th century Chinese writer and translator Lu Xun, who said: "Poetry must have shape, be easy to remember and understand and recite; it must fall easily on the ear, but the form should not be too strict."

The 66 poems chosen by Professor Wu Yansheng posed particular challenges since each one was also a vehicle for a spiritual message that often lay beneath its surface. In translating them I could not have done without the illumination of Professor Wu's commentary. If the poem on the page contradicted the commentary or lacked the qualities of the poem discussed in the commentary then clearly I had failed, however acceptable it may have appeared in English.

Professor Wu's selection is divided between poetry and *gatha*, the poetry generally written by poets who were also Buddhists and the *gatha* by monks who were also poets. The *gatha* form is described by Professor Wu in his introduction. Its function, to stimulate spiritual thought or inculcate Buddhist precepts, in some ways resembles that of the Anglican hymn as a vehicle for doctrine. The *gatha* may be less lyrical than the poetry but it is often more doctrinally profound and more startling and hence stimulating in its imagery. As a very general rule, the reader may identify the distinction between the two forms by the author's name. Buddhist monks, for example, Foyin and Fayan, tend to have just two-character Buddhist names while the secular poets retain their full family name, for example, Tao Yuanming and Bai Juyi.

The translator of Zen poetry gazes on a landscape where the scenery is subtly different, where rocks are more than rocks and where dust is not just dry, scattered earth but a metaphoric representation of worldly travail. Its appreciation requires a different and more spiritual mindset, certainly from the translator and, perhaps, from the reader too.

Tony Blishen

# Index of Poems

189

# Index of Authors

This book is edited and designed by the Editorial Committee of *Cultural China* series.

Text: Wu Yansheng
Translation: Tony Blishen
Cover Image: Tian Xutong
Interior Designer: Wang Wei
Cover Designer: Diane Davies

Copy Editor: Diane Davies
Editor: Zhang Yicong
Editorial Director: Zhang Yicong

Senior Consultants: Sun Yong, Wu Ying, Yang Xinci
Managing Director and Publisher: Wang Youbu

ISBN: 978-1-60220-148-4

Address any comments about *The Power of Enlightenment: Chinese Zen Poems* to:

Better Link Press
99 Park Ave
New York, NY 10016
USA

or

Shanghai Press and Publishing Development Company
F 7 Donghu Road, Shanghai, China (200031)
Email: comments_betterlinkpress@hotmail.com

Printed in China by Shenzhen Donnelley Printing Co., Ltd.

1 3 5 7 9 10 8 6 4 2